# The Northeast

# *The* Northeast

GREENWOOD PRESS
Westport, Connecticut • London

**Library of Congress Cataloging-in-Publication Data**

Creative Media Applications
  How geography affects the United States/Creative Media Applications.
p. cm.
  Summary: Explores the ways in which geography has affected the lives of the people of
the United States.
  Includes bibliographical references (p. ).
  Contents: v.1. Northeast — v.2. Southeast — v.3. Midwest — v.4. West — v.5. Southwest.
  ISBN 0-313-32250–3 (set) — 0-313-32251–1 (Northeast) — 0-313-32252–X (Southeast) —
0-313-32253–8 (Midwest) — 0-313-32254–6 (West) — 0-313-32255–4 (Southwest)
  1. United States — Geography — Juvenile literature. 2. Human geography — United
States — Juvenile literature. 3. United States — History, Local — Juvenile literature.
4. Regionalism — United States — Juvenile literature. [1. United States — Geography.] I.
Creative Media Applications.

E161.3.H69 2002
304.2'0973—dc21                                                                          2002075304

British Library Cataloguing in Publication Data is available.

Library of Congress Catalog Card Number: 2002075304
ISBN:  0-313-32250-3     (set)
         0-313-32251-1     (Northeast)
         0-313-32252-X     (Southeast)
         0-313-32253-8     (Midwest)
         0-313-32254-6     (West)
         0-313-32255-4     (Southwest)

First published in 2002

Greenwood Press, 88 Post Road West, Westport, CT 06881
An imprint of Greenwood Publishing Group, Inc.
www.greenwood.com

Printed in the United States of America

∞™

The paper used in this book complies with the Permanent Paper Standard issued by the
National Information Standards Organization (Z39.48–1984).

10   9   8   7   6   5   4   3   2   1

A Creative Media Applications, Inc. Production
*Writer:* Robin Doak
*Design and Production:* Fabia Wargin Design, Inc.
*Editor:* Matt Levine
*Copyeditor:* Laurie Lieb
*Proofreader:* Tania Bissell
*AP Photo Researcher:* Yvette Reyes
*Consultant:* Dean M. Hanink, Department of Geography,
    University of Connecticut
*Maps:* Ortelius Design

*Photo Credits:*
*Cover:* ©Photodisc, Inc.
AP/Wide World Photographs *pages:* viii, 4, 8, 12, 15, 18, 23, 30, 34, 37, 45, 47, 53, 55, 56, 70,
    73, 83, 85, 86, 97, 105, 106, 109, 110, 117, 121, 123, 125
©CORBIS *pages:* 58, 95
©Bettmann/CORBIS *pages:* 43, 67, 78, 93
©Kelly-Mooney Photography/CORBIS *page:* 91
©Francis C Mayer/CORBIS *page:* 99
Erie Canal Museum, Syracuse, N.Y. *page:* 17

# Contents

# Introduction

The Northeast region of the United States is bordered by the Atlantic Ocean to the east, the Southeastern states to the south, the Midwestern states to the west, and Canada to the north. There are eleven states in the Northeast. Maine, New Hampshire, Vermont, Massachusetts, Connecticut, and Rhode Island are part of a subregion called the New England states. New York, New Jersey, Pennsylvania, Maryland, and Delaware are known as the Middle Atlantic States. The Middle Atlantic subregion also includes Washington, D.C., our nation's capital.

The Northeast is a region of varied landforms, from lofty peaks and rocky hills to fertile valleys and sandy beaches. Two of the most important geographic features of the region are the Appalachian Mountains to the west and the Atlantic Ocean to the east. Both of these features were key elements in the pattern of settlement and development in the Northeast. From the earliest days of human occupation, the Northeast's landforms have affected where people chose to live in the region. The mountains, rivers, valleys, and ocean also affected how people lived— their jobs, methods of transportation, and choices of housing.

The Northeast has a wet climate, with a lot of rain in the spring and plenty of snow in the winter. There are four distinct seasons in the region. Winters are cold, while summers are warm and humid.

*Many places in the Northeast are popular for winter sports. The region twice hosted the Winter Olympics, both times at Lake Placid, New York— first in 1932, and again in 1980.*

# The Northeast Leads the Way

The first people to live in the Northeast region were Native American tribes, including the Algonquian-speaking people. The Algonquian (al-GON-kee-en) were a group of several hundred tribes who lived throughout the Northeast, as well as in some other regions of the United States. Algonquian-speaking tribes included the Algonquin, Narragansett, Lenape, Mohegan, Pequot, and Wampanoag peoples. Another important group was the Iroquois. In the sixteenth century, five Iroquois tribes in the Northeast joined together to form the Iroquois Confederacy.

The bulk of early European settlement in the United States took place in the Northeast. Most of the first Northeastern settlements were British. Of all the early settlements, only two were not British: New Amsterdam, settled by the Dutch in what is now New York, and New Sweden, settled by the Swedish in what is now Delaware. The British began to colonize the region in the early 1600s. By 1664, they controlled the entire Northeast.

The British started out along the seashore and then slowly moved west as the coastal land became more crowded. Today, several port cities of the Northeast are among the most highly populated in the region, including Boston, New York, Philadelphia, and Baltimore. In contrast, other areas, particularly the northernmost sections of the region, are sparsely populated.

Because of the Northeast's early settlement, regional industries had a head start on those in most other areas of the country. Since colonial days, the region has been a center of industries that were vital to our nation's growth. Farming, fishing, and timber were just three of the earliest industries. In the 1800s, the Northeast became a center of manufacturing. All of these industries remain important to the region. Tourism, too, is a key part of the economy in many areas of the Northeast.

# STATE BIRTHDAYS

Many of the earliest settlements in America were founded in the Northeast. Many of the Northeastern states were also among the first to join the new nation, the United States. (The states are listed in alphabetical order.)

| State | Capital | First Permanent Settlement | Date of Statehood | Order of Statehood |
|-------|---------|----------------------------|-------------------|--------------------|
| Connecticut | Hartford | Wethersfield, 1634 | Jan. 9, 1788 | 5 |
| Delaware | Dover | Wilmington, 1638 | Dec. 7, 1778 | 1 |
| Maine | Augusta | Pemaquid, 1625 | Mar. 15, 1820 | 23 |
| Maryland | Annapolis | St. Mary's City, 1634 | Apr. 28, 1788 | 7 |
| Massachusetts | Boston | Plymouth, 1620 | Feb. 6, 1788 | 6 |
| New Hampshire | Concord | Dover, 1623 | June 21, 1788 | 9 |
| New Jersey | Trenton | Bergen, 1660 | Dec. 18, 1788 | 3 |
| New York | Albany | New Amsterdam, 1626 | July 26, 1788 | 11 |
| Pennsylvania | Harrisburg | Tinicum Island, 1643 | Dec. 12, 1787 | 2 |
| Rhode Island | Providence | Providence, 1636 | May 29, 1790 | 13 |
| Vermont | Montpelier | Fort Dummer, 1724 | Mar. 4, 1791 | 14 |

# MORE STATE STATS

The largest state in the Northeast is New York, with over 47,000 square miles of land. The smallest is Rhode Island. Here, the Northeast states are ordered from smallest to largest.

| State | Size (land and water) | Size Rank | Population | State Rank |
|---|---|---|---|---|
| Rhode Island | 1,045 square miles (2,717 square kilometers) | 50 | 1,048,300 | 43 |
| Delaware | 1,955 square miles (5,083 square kilometers) | 49 | 783,600 | 45 |
| Connecticut | 4,845 square miles (12,597 square kilometers) | 48 | 3,045,500 | 29 |
| New Jersey | 7,419 square miles (19,289 square kilometers) | 46 | 8,414,300 | 9 |
| Massachusetts | 7,838 square miles (20,379 square kilometers) | 45 | 6,349,000 | 13 |
| New Hampshire | 8,969 square miles (23,319 square kilometers) | 44 | 1,235,700 | 41 |
| Vermont | 9,249 square miles (24,047 square kilometers) | 43 | 608,800 | 49 |
| Maryland | 9,775 square miles (25,415 square kilometers) | 42 | 5,296,400 | 19 |
| Maine | 30,865 square miles (80,249 square kilometers) | 39 | 1,274,900 | 40 |
| Pennsylvania | 44,820 square miles (119,751 square kilometers) | 32 | 12,281,000 | 6 |
| New York | 47,224 square miles (122,782 square kilometers) | 30 | 18,976,400 | 3 |

NOTE: All metric conversions in this book are approximate.

# Adirondack Mountains

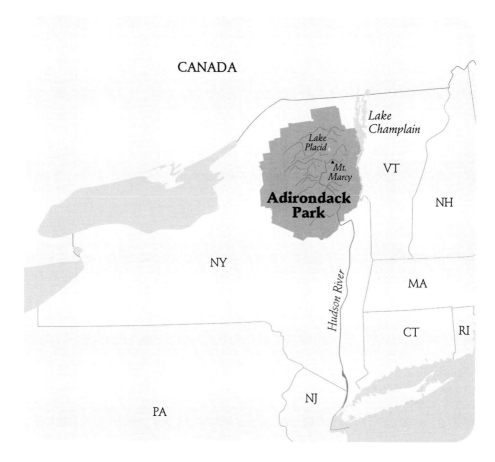

CANADA

Lake
Champlain

Lake
Placid

Mt.
Marcy

VT

NH

**Adirondack
Park**

NY

MA

Hudson River

CT

RI

NJ

PA

**T**he Adirondack (ad-eh-ROHN-dac) Mountains make up an area of heavily forested peaks in northeastern New York. The boundaries of this mountain range are the Canadian border to the north, the Mohawk Valley to the south, the Black River Valley to the west, and Lake Champlain to the east. The highest mountain in the Adirondacks is Mount Marcy, with a height of 5,344 feet (1,603 meters). Mount Marcy is also the highest peak in New York State.

The area that surrounds the mountains is filled with scenic valleys and ridges, as well as lakes, rivers, and waterfalls. The area's lakes include Lake Placid, Lake George, Schroon Lake, and the Upper and Lower Saranacs. Several rivers have their sources in the Adirondacks. The Hudson River, for example, rises in Lake Tear of the Clouds at the top of Mount Marcy.

# A Mountain Is Born

The Adirondacks are sometimes mistakenly thought to be part of the Appalachian mountain system. They are, in fact, part of a geographic region known as the Canadian Shield. The Canadian Shield covers nearly half of Canada, as well as parts of the northern United States. The Canadian Shield is the oldest part of North America's continental plate.

The Adirondack Mountains are made up of some very ancient rocks. Geologists believe that some of the rocks here may be 1.3 billion years old. Although the rocks themselves are old, the mountain peaks are young, geologically speaking. About 59 million years ago, the flat ground of the Adirondack region began to rise. Rocks more than 11 miles (17.6 kilometers) underground were gradually pushed to the surface, and the area eventually took on a large dome shape. Much later, erosion and glaciers carved out the Adirondacks' separate peaks, lakes, and rivers. Geologists say that the mountains continue to rise at the astonishing speed of up to 0.1 inch (0.25 centimeter) per year.

## HOW MOUNT MARCY MEASURES UP

Mount Marcy is the highest mountain in New York. Here's how it compares to some of America's other big peaks.

| Mountain | State | Elevation |
| --- | --- | --- |
| Mount Marcy | New York | 5,344 feet (1,603 meters) |
| Mount St. Helens | Washington | 8,365 feet (2,510 meters) |
| Mount Hood | Oregon | 11,239 feet (3,372 meters) |
| Mount Rainier | Washington | 14,410 feet (4,323 meters) |
| Mount McKinley | Alaska | 20,320 feet (6,096 meters) |

## DID YOU KNOW...?

Some historians think that the word *Adirondacks* comes from an Iroquois term meaning "they who eat trees." The term may have been used by the Iroquois to belittle their enemies, the Algonquin. The first person to use the word Adirondack to describe the mountains was Professor Ebenezer Emmons, a well-known Massachusetts geologist. Emmons surveyed the area in 1838.

*Samuel de Champlain, the first European to explore the Adirondacks, was injured in a battle with the Iroquois. He was carried to safety by his Algonquin guides.*

# Early Inhabitants

The Adirondack area was first settled hundreds of years ago by the Algonquin and Iroquois tribes. Both tribes claimed the Adirondack Mountains as their own for hunting and fishing. The forests of the Adirondacks were rich hunting grounds, filled with deer, moose, and many types of birds. The surrounding lakes and streams teemed with bass, trout, and other fish. Neither tribe ever permanently settled there, however, because the soil of the region was rocky and hard to farm. The mountains acted as a barrier between the two enemy tribes, but the barrier sometimes turned into a bloody battleground.

The first European to explore the region was Frenchman Samuel de Champlain in 1609. Champlain and a number of Algonquin guides entered the Adirondacks from the east, crossing Lake Champlain. When Champlain encountered a large group of Iroquois, he promptly shot several of them. This was the beginning of the Iroquois hatred for the French. The Iroquois refused to trade with the French and later aided the English during the French and Indian War (1754–1763). This war was fought between the English and French. It resulted in the English gaining control of all French holdings east of the Mississippi River except New Orleans.

# Lumber and Mining Industries

More than a century after Champlain, the Adirondacks remained unpopulated. After the American Revolution (1775–1783), veterans were paid off in Adirondack land grants. Few actually settled there, however, since they found the densely forested, rocky terrain and the cold mountain winters unappealing.

In the early 1800s, some people began to look for ways to exploit one of the Adirondacks' most bountiful resources: the trees. White pine, spruce, maple, ash, and hemlock lined the mountains and lakesides. The trees were used to build homes, ships, furniture, and wagons. But potential lumber barons faced one big problem. It was nearly impossible to get the trees off the mountains to the markets in New York City and other trade centers.

Finally, in the spring of 1813, a system was devised to solve the problem. Loggers floated the cut trees one by one down a stream until they reached a larger river.

After this, the trees were driven to a lake, where they were processed in a sawmill. These "river drives" were only the first step to getting the wood to market. Soon canals were constructed to transport the lumber out of the area. By the mid-1800s, New York was the top lumber-producing state in the nation.

Also in the early 1800s, people found another valuable commodity in the Adirondacks: iron ore. Iron was used to make many things, including stoves and bridge cables. Small mining communities popped up in the region. But the miners faced the same transportation problems that the lumber industry had faced. Eventually, iron was found in other, easier-to-reach places, and most of the small mining operations shut down. Today, garnet, zinc, and talc are still mined in the Adirondacks.

One result of the work of the lumber and mining industries was the destruction of some of the Adirondack environment. Lumbering resulted in the deforestation of many areas, while mining polluted nearby waterways. People who loved the Adirondacks' wilderness began to worry that it was being destroyed.

*opposite: Beginning in the early 1800s, many Adirondack trees were cut down and sent to sawmills. Wood from the trees was used to build houses, furniture, and many other wood products.*

## Tourism Takes Off

One of the most important chapters in Adirondack history began in 1869. That year, a popular book about the Adirondacks' natural beauty began to attract many wealthy tourists to the area. Between 1870 and 1910, people like J.P. Morgan, William Rockefeller, and Alfred Vanderbilt built what came to be called "Great Camps." With sixty buildings, Vanderbilt's Great Camp was a minivillage. It came equipped with staff quarters, guest homes for visiting royalty or movie stars, and even a bowling alley and casino.

Soon the Adirondacks had become the "in" place to spend the summer. Luxury hotels sprang up in the area to cater to the ever increasing numbers of tourists. Train service, which had originally been built to serve the lumber industry, expanded to shuttle passengers in and out of the region. Steamboats cruised the lakes, ferrying hotel guests to and from the train station. The Adirondacks had become a tourist attraction.

*Increased tourism created a need for more roads through the Adirondacks. In 1935, the Veterans Memorial Highway opened to take people to the top of Whiteface Mountain in New York.*

### "TAKING THE CURE" IN THE ADIRONDACKS

Dr. Edward Livingston Trudeau, suffering from tuberculosis, first traveled from New York City to the Adirondacks in 1873. Over the next few years, Trudeau came to believe that the rest and fresh air he enjoyed in the mountains were a cure for his disease. In 1884, near Saranac Lake, he founded the first sanatorium in the United States for people with tuberculosis. A *sanatorium* is a place where people go to be treated for an illness. People traveled from around the world to "take the cure" in the Adirondacks.

After World War I (1914–1918), winter activities became a popular tourist draw in the Adirondacks. Skiing, skating, and sleigh riding attracted visitors, even in the coldest winters. Lake Placid became the center of world attention in 1932 and again in 1980 when it hosted the Winter Olympic Games. Today, tourism still plays an important role in the region. Hikers, skiers, and nature lovers venture to the wilderness to enjoy the Adirondacks' raw beauty.

# Preserving a Natural Treasure

More than a hundred years ago, people recognized the need to preserve the Adirondack region for future generations. To that end, Adirondack Park was established in 1892. Today, the park covers more than 6 million acres (2.4 million hectares), making it the largest state park in the continental United States.

The park has yet another distinction: More than half of the land is owned by private landowners. Sometimes the interests of the landowners clash with the interests of people who want to preserve the park as it is. The largest landowners, for example, are paper companies. They want to be able to keep cutting trees on their land. Private citizens want to be able to build on their land and use the land as they see fit. Yet some strict regulations may prevent them from doing so. Balancing public and private interests remains a challenge in Adirondack Park.

The Adirondack region faces another serious problem: acid rain. Acid rain is caused by emissions of sulfur dioxide and other gases into the atmosphere. Sulfur dioxide is released into the air through car exhausts, as well as factory emissions. Researchers say that as many as 350 Adirondack lakes and ponds can no longer support fish and other life because of acid rain. Forests at the highest elevations are also in danger. In recent years, federal and state laws have been passed to try to curb the emission of pollutants that cause acid rain. Only time will tell if the laws are successful.

## PRESIDENTIAL CONNECTIONS

- Theodore Roosevelt was climbing Mount Marcy in 1901 when he learned that President William McKinley was dying from an assassin's bullet. Roosevelt rushed down the mountain, and the next day he became the twenty-sixth president of the United States.
- In 1926, the thirtieth president, Calvin Coolidge, established a summer White House at one of the Great Camps in the Adirondacks.
- As New York's governor, Franklin Roosevelt opened the Winter Olympic Games at Lake Placid in 1932. Later that year, Roosevelt was elected thirty-second president of the United States.

# Appalachian Mountains

## 2

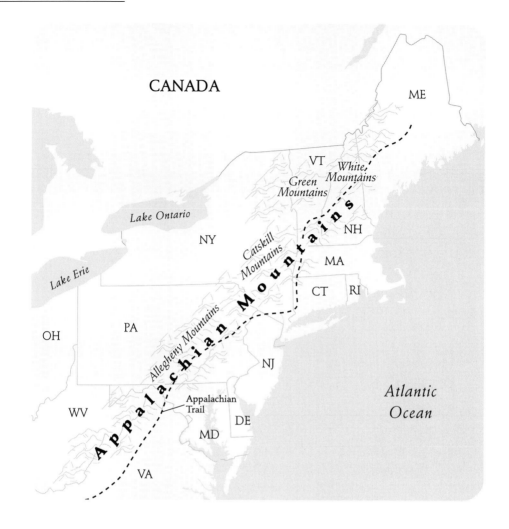

T
he Appalachian (ap-eh-LAY-shen) Mountains
in eastern North America make up one of
the largest mountain systems on the
continent. Only the Rocky Mountains are
larger. The Appalachians stretch more than 1,600 miles
(2,560 kilometers), paralleling the Atlantic Coast from
central Alabama all the way to Newfoundland,
Canada. In the northeast region, they pass through
Maine, Vermont, New Hampshire, New York,
Massachusetts, Connecticut, Pennsylvania, New
Jersey, Maryland, and Delaware.

The ancient Appalachian peaks are thickly
forested and rounded from thousands of years of

erosion. The highest peak in the entire mountain system, Mount Mitchell in North Carolina, is 6,684 feet (2,005 meters) high. The tallest mountain in the northeastern region of the Appalachians is Mount Washington in New Hampshire. At 6,288 feet (1,886 meters), Washington towers above all other mountains in New England.

On a map, the Appalachians look like one long, narrow mountain chain, but they can be divided into separate mountain groups. In the Northeast, these groups include the Green, White, Catskill, and Allegheny Mountains. Many rivers run through the northeastern Appalachians. The largest of these are the Hudson, Mohawk, Delaware, Susquehanna, Potomac, and James Rivers.

## MOUNTAIN RANGES OF THE APPALACHIANS

On a map, the Appalachians look like one continuous chain of mountains, but they are actually made up of several smaller groups of mountains. The mountain groups in the northeastern Appalachians are as follows.

| Range | States | Highest Mountain and Elevation |
|---|---|---|
| Green Mountains | Vermont | Mount Mansfield, 4,393 feet (1,318 meters) |
| White Mountains | New Hampshire, Maine | Mount Washington, 6,288 feet (1,886 meters) |
| Berkshire Hills | Massachusetts, Connecticut, New York | Mount Greylock, 3,491 feet (1,047 meters) |
| Catskill Mountains | New York | Slide Mountain, 4,202 feet (1,261 meters) |
| Allegheny Mountains | Pennsylvania, Maryland, *Virginia, *West Virginia | Spruce Knob, 4,860 feet (1,458 meters) |

* Not Northeastern states

# Geological History of the Appalachians

Geologists believe that the Appalachians are the oldest mountain system in the United States, possibly twice as old as the Rockies. The mountains first began forming about 450 million years ago. The building process continued until about 250 million years ago.

When the Appalachian Mountains were first formed, their peaks were much higher and more pointed. Eventually, more than 200 million years of erosion wore the mountains down to the size that they are now. In the northern Appalachians, heavy glaciers also played an important role, squeezing and compressing the land under tons of ice. Today, visitors to New England can see big boulders and rocks, evidence of the glaciers that were there more than a million years ago.

## APPALACHIAN ORIGINS

The term *Appalachian* comes from the name of a Native American tribe in northern Florida: the Apalachee. Sixteenth-century Spanish explorers were the first to call the massive mountains by that name. Some believe the term means "helper" or "ally." Others think it means "people on the other side."

# Settlement in the Appalachians

Native American tribes were living in the Appalachian area for centuries before Europeans first settled in North America. Northeastern Appalachian tribes included the Micmac, Seneca, Mohawk, Susquehannock (suss-kwa-HAN-uck), and Lenape. Most of the tribes settled in the fertile valley regions of the Appalachians; the land closer to the mountains was too hard and rocky for successful farming. The densely forested mountain areas were used mainly for hunting.

As European settlers began to arrive in the northeast, they claimed the foothills and valleys near the mountains as their own. The native people were

slowly pushed farther and farther into the
Appalachians. By the 1700s, most Native Americans
had been moved off their fertile farmland.

*The Appalachians seemed like an insurmountable barrier to early settlers.*

Permanent settlements and towns sprang up in the
mountain valleys, especially along the banks of the
rivers that ran out of the Appalachians. The rivers
served as a means of transporting goods between the
mountains and the coast. Settlers also constructed
mills and built up other industries near the rivers.

As more and more settlers arrived from Europe,
the valleys and coastal areas became crowded.
Beginning in the early 1700s, those seeking land of
their own began to move closer to the mountains. By
the mid-1800s, settlers had cleared most of the eastern
Appalachian forestland for homes and farms. They
soon learned a lesson that the natives had known: The
rocky soil was not easy to cultivate.

For the European settlers, the Appalachian
Mountains at first were a natural barrier to the west.

The towering mountains seemed impassable to most of the early immigrants. It wasn't until the mid-1700s that pioneers finally blazed a trail through the mountains. As the western frontier across the mountains began to open up, many Appalachian farmers abandoned their land and headed west in search of better farmland.

# Over the Mountains

In the late 1700s, frontiersmen began looking for a way to get to the land west of the Appalachians. In the Northeast, one of the first roads through the mountains was Braddock's Road. Braddock's Road, opened in 1755 during the French and Indian War (1754–1763), was little more than a narrow horse trail from Cumberland, Maryland, to Pittsburgh, Pennsylvania. The winding path was named for British Major General Edward Braddock, who was buried in the road during the war. A second, better-traveled road was opened just three years later. The Forbes Road, blazed in 1758 by Brigadier General John Forbes, was one of the most common routes for settlers traveling west from the Northeast. The road ended in present-day Pittsburgh.

**HENRY HUDSON**

Dutch explorer Henry Hudson was the first European to set foot in the Catskill Mountains of New York. In 1609, Hudson made his third trip to North America in an attempt to find the Northwest Passage from the Atlantic Ocean to the Pacific Ocean. He journeyed into the mountains that he called the Catskills, from the Dutch word *kaaterskill*, or "wildcat creek."

In 1763, the British government forbade colonists from settling west of the Appalachians. The western land was meant to be the territory of the Native Americans. However, the order was soon rescinded, and many people settled there. The majority of early settlers who worked their way across the Appalachians to western Pennsylvania were German and Scotch-Irish.

# By Boat and by Train

As more and more people began to settle west of the Appalachians, there was a greater demand for goods to be shipped back and forth. However, the Appalachians were still an obstacle. Although there were trails, it was still difficult to transport goods across the rocky, rugged mountains. On July 4, 1817, New York State began constructing a canal through the Appalachians. The plan was to dig a waterway that would connect Lake Erie and the other Great Lakes to the Atlantic coast.

*Men operate manual pulley cranes to dig the Erie Canal lock at Lockport, New York.*

## A GRAND CANAL

When the Erie Canal was completed, it was 363 miles (581 kilometers) long, 40 feet (12 meters) wide, and an average of 4 feet (1.2 meters) deep. The Erie Canal was a towpath canal. Canal boats were tied to mules or horses that walked on paths along the banks of the canal and towed the boats from one station to another.

The first boat to travel the canal was the *Seneca Chief*, on October 26, 1825. By the 1830s, there were more than 3,000 canal boats operating on the Erie Canal.

Before the canal opened, it cost $100 to ship a ton (0.9 metric ton) of goods from New York City to Buffalo. After, the price dropped by about 90 percent.

*A boat waits at a canal dock in Syracuse, New York, in the early 1900s. Similar boats moved freight up and down the Erie Canal from 1825 until that time.*

The Erie Canal took eight years and more than $7 million to complete. Thousands of workers, most of them Irish and German immigrants, toiled for $10 a month to dig the big canal. The canal helped New York City maintain its status as the number one port and trade center in the country. In 1834, Pennsylvania followed New York's lead, building the Pennsylvania Canal to connect Philadelphia and Pittsburgh.

Canals were the most important mode of transportation across the northern Appalachians for a short time. In the 1850s, five different railroad lines were built to cross the Appalachians. Because of the speed and comfort of the train, the railway soon became the preferred way of traveling. Much later, the automobile and paved highways cut through the Appalachians. A crossing that once took weeks now takes just hours.

## Appalachian Economics

The Appalachian Mountains played an important role in the Northeast's economy. Both the New England and Middle Atlantic states were dependent upon the mountains in many ways. Farming, lumbering, and mining all helped the Northeast—and America—grow and thrive.

Farming, important to the Native Americans of the region thousands of years ago, was also important to the earliest European settlers. In the fertile valleys of the northeast Appalachians, farmers grew apples, potatoes, hay, wheat, and barley. Dairy farms were also established in the hills and valleys. Today, farming is still an essential part of the Appalachian area economy.

# The Lumber Industry

The first major industry associated with the Appalachians was the lumber industry. Timbering was especially important to the northern New England states. In the 1600s, the British were the first to realize the wealth that lay within the mountains' vast hardwood forests. White pines grew strong and straight. The British wanted to use these trees for shipbuilding and other ventures.

In 1691, British soldiers began to mark the best white pines with a large *V* that signified government property. These trees became known as "Broad Arrow Trees" and the "King's Pine." Eventually, angry colonists fought for the right to cut their own trees. In 1772, New Hampshire sawmill owners attacked a sheriff who tried to enforce King George III's edict. The attack, which became known as the Pine Tree Riot, was one of the first open acts of rebellion against England. The King's Pine issue is said to be one of the reasons that New Englanders so quickly rebelled against the British.

In the early 1800s, the lumber industry flourished. Wood was one of the most important products in the growing nation. It was needed to build ships, homes, and other items. Wood was also needed as fuel for heating, so timber was heavily in demand.

Lumbering was a year-round business. In the wintertime, lumberjacks cut and piled logs on top of frozen rivers and streams. In the spring, when the ice melted, the logs would be carried down from the mountains in huge "river drives."

Lumberjacking was a dangerous occupation. Many men were injured or killed by falling branches or trees. River drives were particularly risky. Log drivers carefully watched tons of 16-foot (4.8-meter) logs racing down pounding rivers and streams. If the logs became jammed together, it was up to the driver to get in there and separate them. Some log drivers were crushed or drowned during river drives.

Logging was so widespread in the northeastern Appalachians that by the early twentieth century, three-quarters of all the white pine trees had been cut down. In some parts of the Appalachian Mountains, only a tiny percentage of old-growth forest was left standing. *Old-growth forests* are forests that have been growing for many, many years. They have a well-developed ecosystem that includes unique types of trees, plants, and wildlife. Destroying old-growth forests also destroys these ecosystems. Although the Appalachians are not logged as extensively as they once were, timber, pulp, and paper industries are still important in New England, especially in northern Maine.

# Coal Mining in Pennsylvania

In Pennsylvania, another Appalachian industry began to take hold after the Civil War (1861–1865): coal mining. Coal had been discovered in the Appalachian area in the 1700s, but it had not been mined extensively. There was no widespread use for the mineral. That changed in the 1860s, with the advent of the steam engine. Coal became a much needed commodity to power these engines.

The coal mined in the Appalachians gave U.S. industries a big boost. In addition to powering steam engines, coal also provided the fuel for plants that produced the nation's electricity. Coal boosted Pennsylvania's economy, too. The state's steel industry, in particular, benefited from

## THE HARWICK EXPLOSION

One of the worst coal mining disasters in U.S. history took place on January 25, 1904, in a small town near Pittsburgh, Pennsylvania. That morning, an explosion at the Harwick Mine killed 179 people. Two more men were later killed trying to rescue the injured. Only one person who was in the mine at the time survived the blast.

coal. Coal-fired steel furnaces made Pittsburgh the steel center of the world.

Coal mining was hard work that paid poorly. Many of the workers were immigrants from eastern and southern European countries. In some mines, children as young as seven years old were sent to work. Many of the miners and their families lived in company towns that sprang up around the mines. Here, workers lived in company-owned homes and bought their food and supplies at company-owned stores.

## THE NATION'S FIRST OIL WELL

The nation's first commercial oil well was drilled in the Appalachians. In 1859, Edwin L. Drake struck oil 69 feet (20.7 meters) below the surface of Titusville, Pennsylvania. For decades after his find, Pennsylvania was the top oil producer in the nation.

Mining coal was dangerous, too. Since 1870, more than 50,000 people have died in mining accidents in Pennsylvania alone. Thousands of others have been killed by black lung disease, a condition caused by breathing in coal dust. The terrible state of early coal mines led to the rise of labor unions in the area. The mines also led to an outcry against child labor around the nation.

However, coal mining remained a major industry in Pennsylvania until the 1950s, when oil and natural gas began to displace coal as a fuel source. Today, people are once again turning to coal as an alternative fuel. Because of safety regulations, mining today is much safer than it was decades ago.

Coal mining has left a mark on the Appalachian environment itself. One of the longest-lasting effects is the pollution of streams and rivers, caused by acid mine drainage. Runoff from the coal-mining process has killed fish and other wildlife that live in the waters. Conservationists are working to find a solution to this problem.

# The Appalachians and Tourism

Another industry has recently become important in the Appalachians. Each year, thousands of tourists travel to the mountains from all around the world. In New York, Catskill State Park has breathtaking waterfalls, peaks, and caves. The Green Mountains of Vermont are famous for their many ski resorts, including Stowe and Killington. And the White Mountains of New Hampshire boast some of the tallest, most scenic peaks in New England.

*Earl Shaffer completed his third "thru-hike" of the 2,150-mile (3,440-kilometer) Appalachian Trail in 1998 at the age of 79. He says the trail is "a series of obstacle courses."*

## • Fast Fact •

The Appalachian Trail is actually longer than the entire Appalachian Mountain Range.

For hikers and backpackers, a highlight of the Appalachians is the Appalachian National Scenic Trail. The Appalachian Trail is the nation's longest marked footpath, extending more than 2,000 miles (3,200 kilometers). The trail begins at Springer Mountain in Georgia and continues to Mount Katahdin in Maine.

## THE PRESIDENTIAL RANGE

The White Mountains of New Hampshire are home to some of the tallest mountains in New England. The Presidential Range, part of the White Mountains, includes peaks named for our first five presidents.

| Mountain | Elevation |
|---|---|
| Mount Washington | 6,288 feet (1,886 meters) |
| Mount Adams | 5,798 feet (1,739 meters) |
| Mount Jefferson | 5,715 feet (1,715 meters) |
| Mount Monroe | 5,385 feet (1,616 meters) |
| Mount Madison | 5,363 feet (1,609 meters) |

# Atlantic Ocean

**3**

The Atlantic Ocean is one of the most important geographical features that affects the Northeast. Throughout our nation's history, the Atlantic has played a pivotal role in the development and growth of the region. It has served as a route for settlers, traders, and soldiers. The bays, inlets, rivers, and islands all along the Atlantic coast have facilitated the growth of some of the busiest, most thriving cities in the world. And the ocean's shores have become a gateway for people seeking a new life.

Nearly 32 million square miles (83.2 million square kilometers) in size, the Atlantic Ocean is the second-largest ocean in the world. Only the Pacific Ocean is larger. In the Northeast, the Atlantic coastline extends nearly 800 miles (1,280 kilometers) from northern

Maine to southern Maryland. The tidal shoreline of the Northeast, which includes islands, bays, inlets, and *estuaries* (places where salt water from the ocean mixes with fresh water from streams and rivers), is more than 13,400 miles (21,440 kilometers) long.

The Atlantic Ocean has shaped the northeastern coastline over many, many years. Wind and waves created the narrow, rocky beaches in the north and the long, sandy stretches in the south. The Atlantic continues to shape the shoreline even today, as wind and water erode rock and sand, gradually washing away beaches, islands, and even houses.

The climate near the shore is generally more moderate than it is further inland. In the summer, temperatures are cooler; in the winter, temperatures are warmer. The mild climate is just one reason that people are attracted to life on the coast. Today, 50 percent of all Americans live within 50 miles (80 kilometers) of an ocean.

## THE YOUNGEST OCEAN

Formed only about 200 million years ago, the Atlantic is the youngest of all oceans. The word *Atlantic* may come from Atlantis, a legendary island that was said to have sunk into the sea thousands of years ago.

## OCEAN STATS

The world's three major oceans are the Pacific, Atlantic, and Indian Oceans. Here's how they compare to one another in size and depth.

| Ocean | Size | Percent of Earth Covered | Average Depth |
|---|---|---|---|
| Pacific | 63,800,000 square miles (165,880,000 square kilometers) | 32% | 13,215 feet (3,965 meters) |
| Atlantic | 31,800,000 square miles (82,680,000 square kilometers) | 16% | 12,880 feet (3,864 meters) |
| Indian | 28,900,000 square miles (75,140,000 square kilometers) | 15% | 13,002 feet (3,901 meters) |

# Settlement along the Northeast Coast

The first people to settle along the Atlantic coast in the Northeast were ancestors of later Native American tribes. Thousands of years ago, these people traveled across a land bridge that at one time connected Asia to North America. Before the first Europeans arrived, the largest group was the Algonquian-speaking tribes. These tribes included the Algonquin, Micmac, Penobscot, Wampanoag, and Lenape. The natives used the Atlantic as a food source, taking fish, clams, mussels, oysters, and lobsters from the cold water.

Vikings explored and briefly settled on the northeast Atlantic coast as early as A.D. 1000. However, the first permanent European settlement in the Northeast was established in Plymouth,

## EARLY ARRIVALS

Before the Pilgrims arrived in 1620, many other explorers charted the coasts of the Northeast. Here are a few of them.

| Explorer | Country | Year | Area Explored |
|---|---|---|---|
| Leif Eriksson | Scandinavia | A.D. 1000 | Somewhere between Newfoundland and Virginia |
| Giovanni da Verrazano | France | 1524 | Northeast coastline |
| Estevan Gomez | Spain | 1525 | Entire Atlantic coast |
| Bartholomew Gosnold | Great Britain | 1602 | Maine, Massachusetts |
| Samuel de Champlain | France | 1604 | Maine, Massachusetts |
| Henry Hudson | Netherlands | 1609 | New York |
| Adriaen Block | Netherlands | 1613 | New York, Connecticut |
| John Smith | Great Britain | 1614 | New England |

Massachusetts, in 1620. That December, a group of Puritans seeking religious freedom from England established a community near Cape Cod. These first settlers became known as the Pilgrims.

For the earliest British settlers, the ocean served as a link to Great Britain. Ships carrying newcomers, goods, and news from home began traversing the Atlantic between the Old and New Worlds. Little more than ten years after the Pilgrims arrived, about 1,600 Europeans made their home in the Massachusetts Colony. In another ten years, 20,000 more would take their chances in the New World.

The first settlements in many states of the Northeast were founded along the Atlantic coast. Settlements up and down the coastline thrived as more people arrived from Europe. These coastal cities included Portsmouth, New Hampshire (founded in 1623); New Amsterdam, New York (1626); Boston, Massachusetts (1630); Portland, Maine (1632); Providence, Rhode Island (1638); and Annapolis, Maryland (1649). Gradually, as the coast became more crowded, settlers moved inland.

Throughout our nation's history, people from other nations poured into the Atlantic port cities looking for a better life. In the 1800s, millions of immigrants came into the nation through such ports of entry as Boston and New York. Some remained in the cities; others moved westward, into our nation's interior.

# Fishing and Whaling

For Native Americans and the earliest settlers, fishing in the Atlantic Ocean was a way to provide food for themselves and their families. Colonists discovered that the northern Atlantic provided a rich fishing ground, filled with cod, sole, haddock, crabs, clams, mussels, and lobsters. Soon, fishing became one of the first Northeast industries.

## HURRICANE TERRITORY

Living along the Atlantic coast carries risks, as well as benefits. Hurricanes—gigantic, killer storms—pose serious threats. New England, jutting out into the Atlantic Ocean, is especially at risk. Since the 1600s, hurricanes in New England have destroyed buildings and homes, wiped out fishing industries, and caused the deaths of many people.

- August 1635: *The Great Colonial Hurricane*
  The first recorded hurricane in New England sank ships, destroyed homes, and killed at least twenty-one people.

- September 1815: *The Great September Gale*
  The storm ripped through New England, destroying buildings and trees. Six people were killed. It is considered the second-worst hurricane in New England history.

- September 1938: *The Great New England Hurricane*
  This was the worst hurricane in New England history. Homes along the coast were destroyed and swept out to sea. The storm caused the deaths of 600 people and wreaked more than $300 million in damages.

- August 1955: *Hurricane Diane*
  Diane caused some of the worst flooding ever seen, resulting in more than $1.5 billion in damages.

During the early colonial days, fishermen sold their catch to merchants in the larger ports, including Boston and Salem, Massachusetts. The merchants dried the fish and exported it to Europe and the West Indies. As the demands for Atlantic fish increased, other industries, such as shipbuilding, evolved. By the end of the 1600s, fishing had become the backbone of New England commerce.

Some communities were settled because of fishing. In 1623, people who wanted to be near the rich fishing grounds in the North Atlantic founded Gloucester, Massachusetts. Gloucester is the oldest fishing port in the United States, and fishing continues there today.

The Isles of Shoals, a group of nine small rocky islands off the coast of New Hampshire, was another fishing community settled by fishers and their families. By the end of the 1600s, more than 300 people lived and fished off the desolate, hostile islands. People eventually moved away as fishing ports on the mainland became more prosperous.

The Atlantic coast fishing industry continues to be important to the economy in the Northeast. In recent years, however, overfishing in some areas has caused the depletion of many types of fish, especially in the New England fishing grounds.

*opposite:*
*The Hurricane of 1938 pounded the Commercial Fisheries building in Woods Hole, Massachusetts. Six hundred people lost their lives in this storm.*

## The Whaling Industry

Colonists were whaling in the Northeast as early as the 1600s. Settlers on Long Island and Cape Cod were taught how to hunt whales by the native people of the area. In the early 1700s, mass whaling began in the Atlantic Ocean. At that time, it was discovered that whale oil could be used to light lamps in homes and lighthouses, as well as to make soap, paint, and even margarine.

Nantucket, Massachusetts, was one of the first—and for a time, the busiest—whaling ports in the nation. During the early 1800s, however, another Northeast town became known as the "whaling capital of the world." New Bedford, Massachusetts, was founded in the 1760s by a Nantucket whaler looking for a new, less crowded port to sail from. In 1845 alone, 10,000 men shipped out of New Bedford on whaling trips.

Whaling, like other types of fishing, was a dangerous, exhausting task. Voyages could last for up to four years as ships sailed to the South Pacific and the Arctic in search of gray, right, and sperm whales. Some of the men who began the voyage never returned, victims of shipwrecks, drowning, onboard diseases, or accidents while hunting the whales.

In 1859, oil was discovered in Pennsylvania, spelling the end of the whaling industry in New Bedford and other ports. After whaling, New Bedford turned to textiles, becoming one of the largest mill towns in the Northeast. New Bedford's excellent harbor and access to shipping routes made it a desirable location for mills. The textile industry drew French Canadian, Portuguese, and Italian immigrants as workers.

**DOWN TO THE SEA**

Since the early 1700s, thousands of Gloucester's fishermen have been lost at sea. In just one month in 1879, sixteen vessels and more than 160 men who shipped out of Gloucester died at sea.

## Shipping and Shipbuilding

Shipping is another important industry in the Northeast. Some of the first merchants along the Atlantic shoreline were called "coasters." Coasters traveled up and down the coast, selling produce and other goods at one settlement after another. The coasters also linked the port towns, bringing news and gossip along with their wares. The largest harbors, such as Boston and New York, attracted many coasters. Coasters continued to sell their wares up and down the Atlantic coast until the middle of the nineteenth century, when steamships and railroads finally put them out of business.

Eventually, merchants began to look outside of the colonies to make money. In 1642, a Boston merchant loaded his ship with fish and barrel staves and headed to the Azores, an archipelago west of Portugal. The captain traded his goods for wine and sugar. On the way home, he stopped in the West Indies to pick up cotton, tobacco, and iron. After selling his goods at home, the merchant had made a tidy profit.

This marked the beginning of what came to be called "triangular trade." A ship would set sail from its home port loaded with goods. These goods would be traded for different wares at a second port. The ship would then journey on to a third, and sometimes a fourth or fifth port, repeating the buying and selling process.

Triangular trade began to take on a more sinister reputation in the late 1600s, when the first stop on many journeys became the west coast of Africa. Here, rum from the colonies was traded for slaves. The slaves were taken to the West Indies and exchanged for sugar and molasses.

## *MOBY DICK*

Herman Melville wrote the classic novel *Moby Dick* in 1851. This story of a huge white whale and an obsessed sea captain is one of the greatest adventure tales of all time. Melville's knowledge of whaling came from firsthand experience: In 1841, he sailed from New Bedford, Massachusetts, on the whaler *Acushnet*. After eighteen months on board, Melville deserted in the Marquesas Islands in the South Pacific.

## PIRATES OF NEW ENGLAND

People who lived in coastal settlements had to be on the lookout for pirates. In addition to stopping ships at sea, pirates sometimes raided shoreline towns. One of the earliest pirates sailing the Atlantic was Dixie Bull, who attacked trading posts and trading vessels in 1623. Other famous pirates who terrorized New England waters include Black Sam Bellamy, William Kidd, Rachel Wall, and Edward Teach—more commonly known as Blackbeard.

*In this portrait, the notorious pirate Blackbeard (Edward Teach) is shown carrying the weapons of his trade while his men load a longboat with supplies or plunder.*

One of the top slaving ports in the Atlantic coast colonies was Newport, Rhode Island. In the 1760s, at the peak of the slave trade, there were more than 180 slave ships operating out of that port city. Slavery was banned in Rhode Island shortly before the start of the American Revolution (1775–1783).

After the American Revolution, U.S. merchants were free to trade wherever they liked. In the early 1790s, traders out of Boston and Salem began voyaging to China. They brought back tea, silk, cotton, bamboo furniture, coffee, ginger, and pepper.

# Shipbuilding Takes Off

Such industries as fishing, whaling, and commerce led to another staple of the Northeast economy—shipbuilding. Not only were there plenty of places to build boats, but the nearby forests guaranteed a steady supply of lumber. Shipbuilders in the colonies began making boats that were much less expensive than those made in Great Britain.

One important shipbuilding town in the Northeast was Boston. In the seventeenth and eighteenth centuries, Boston was filled with shipyards. Secondary businesses also benefited from the shipbuilding boom. Coopers (barrel makers), carpenters, rope makers, and sail makers all found plenty of work to keep them busy. As Boston become overcrowded with shipyards, boat builders moved to the Connecticut River, Rhode Island, Maine, and other coastal areas.

Shipbuilding is still an important industry in the Northeast. In Bath, Maine, workers build battleships and other big boats. Groton, Connecticut, is known as the Submarine Capital of the World. The first sub in Groton was built in 1910. In 1954, the *Nautilus*, the world's first nuclear submarine, was launched from there.

# The Sea Road to Revolution

Although colonial shipping and shipbuilding were a boon to the Northeast's economy, Great Britain viewed these industries as dangerous to its own economic welfare. The more the colonies traded with other countries, the less important Great Britain would become. In a matter of decades, America had already become much more self-sufficient.

As early as 1660, Great Britain attempted to impose trade restrictions and taxes on the colonies. In the 1700s, Great Britain taxed sugar and molasses coming from the West Indies, as well as glass, lead, paint, paper, and tea. These taxes angered colonists, and the rumblings of independence began.

With the start of the American Revolution, shipping and fishing centers were at risk of attack by the British. In late 1776, Great Britain prohibited all trade with America and began blockading port towns. Shore towns were raided and fishing and other vessels burned or confiscated. Colonists were taken off some American ships and imprisoned or forced to fight for the British.

# Protecting the Coast

Less than a year before the colonies declared their independence from Great Britain, they began forming a navy to defend their coast. The decision turned out to be a prudent one: During both the American Revolution and the War of 1812 (1812–1815), the northern Atlantic coast was the site of many naval battles.

The first navy was a little one, formed to raid British ships carrying supplies for the British army. Made up of small ships, the Continental navy did not attack the larger British battleships. One of the great triumphs for the navy during the American Revolution was the capture of the British ship *Drake* by John Paul Jones and the crew of the *Ranger*.

During the War of 1812, the importance of a strong naval presence was driven home as the British raided and burned cities and towns up and down the Atlantic coast. Even though it had a number of battleships, including the *Constitution*, the *United States*, and the *Chesapeake*, the U.S. Navy could do little to stop its enemies. Not even Washington, D.C., escaped British torches. Once the war was over, the United States began building a larger, stronger navy.

*Clamming is a traditional pastime along the Atlantic coast, as well as an important coastal industry.*

## Tourism and Preservation

The cool breezes and sandy beaches along the Atlantic coast have been a draw for visitors and tourists since the 1800s. As people began to have more leisure time, as well as more money to spend, many of them turned to the Atlantic coast to relax.

One well-known Atlantic coast resort is Newport, Rhode Island. By the early twentieth century, the rich of America had made Newport the "in" place to spend the summer. The Vanderbilts, Astors, and Morgans all built summer "cottages" by the seashore. These opulent mansions were more like castles than cottages. Today, the mansions are tourist attractions.

Another coastal attraction is Atlantic City, New Jersey. Atlantic City was founded in 1854 so that people in nearby cities could have a place to go and forget their troubles. The city featured the first ocean boardwalk, amusement rides, and saltwater taffy— even the first Miss America pageant. Today, Atlantic City is a mecca for gamblers, with many casinos filling the tiny, eleven-square-mile town.

As development increased, people became concerned that the wild side of the Atlantic coast would be forever lost. In 1961, the first national seashore was created in Cape Cod, Massachusetts. In addition, all states that border the ocean have established state parks along parts of their coastline.

## NATIONAL SEASHORES IN THE NORTHEAST

| Seashore | State | Protected Area |
|---|---|---|
| Cape Cod (1961) | Massachusetts | 30 miles (48 kilometers) |
| Fire Island (1964) | New York | 32 miles (51.2 kilometers) |
| Assateague Island (1965) | Maryland and Virginia | 37 miles (59.2 kilometers) |

# Cape Cod

**4**

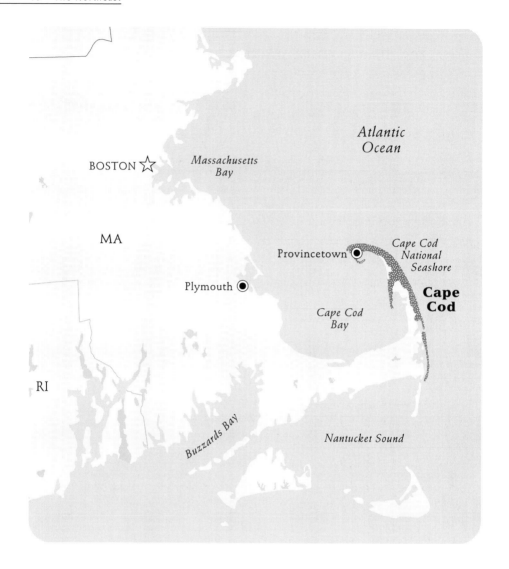

Atlantic
Ocean

BOSTON ☆   Massachusetts
            Bay

MA

Provincetown ◉   Cape Cod
                  National
                  Seashore

Plymouth ◉        **Cape
                  Cod**

Cape Cod
Bay

RI

Buzzards Bay

Nantucket Sound

**C**ape Cod is a peninsula 65 miles (104 kilometers) long in southeastern Massachusetts that juts into the Atlantic Ocean. The region closest to the mainland is sometimes called the Upper Cape. The northernmost tip, where Provincetown is located, is called the Lower, or Outer Cape. In between the two lies the Middle Cape.

Cape Cod's coastline is marked by coves, shallow-water harbors, beaches, dunes, and cliffs. The waters of Cape Cod Bay, along the cape's inner shore, are calm and safe. The outer shore, however, is a different matter. The Atlantic waters off the cape are famous for being treacherous to mariners. Shoals, currents, and sandbars are all dangers in these waters. The cape's interior lands include lakes, forests, ponds, and salt marshes.

## History of the Cape

The Cape Cod peninsula was formed about 25,000 years ago by Ice Age glaciers. Since then, the cape has been shaped by wind and water. Erosion has worn down some areas while building up others. In fact, the face of the cape is still changing. Every year, it loses some of its dunes, cliffs, and beaches to the relentless ocean. Some geologists believe that Cape Cod may be completely covered by water in three or four centuries.

The first humans to make their home on the cape were people who had migrated from Asia during the Pleistocene Epoch. Ancestors of later Native American tribes, they settled along the cape about 11,000 years ago. Before any European settlers found their way to Cape Cod, the Wampanoags lived in the area. The Wampanoags were a group of five or six tribes who lived off the land and the sea. They planted corn and other crops and fished in the coastal waters.

Although Vikings may have explored the cape 1,000 years ago, the first known explorer to visit Cape Cod was Giovanni da Verrazano in 1524. Verrazano, an Italian in the service of France, explored the cape's southwestern shoreline near Buzzards Bay for several weeks.

### NAMING THE CAPE

In 1602, Bartholomew Gosnold anchored off the northern tip of Cape Cod, now known as Provincetown Harbor. Gosnold was impressed with the bountiful supply of codfish he saw in the water. He called the area "Cape Cod," a name that has stuck ever since.

In 1602, Englishman Bartholomew Gosnold arrived at the cape. Although he built a house on an island off the cape, Gosnold did not remain. Two years later, Samuel de Champlain explored Cape Cod's coastline. Champlain created charts and maps of the area to help future adventurers.

# The Pilgrims in Provincetown

On November 21, 1620, 101 people who would become the first permanent settlers in the Northeast anchored off the northern tip of Cape Cod. The passengers, later called the Pilgrims, had braved a ten-week journey from Southampton, England. After sending out a party of men to explore the area, the Pilgrims decided that the land was far too sandy for farming. They got back in their ship, the *Mayflower*, drew up anchor, and sailed across Cape Cod Bay to the mainland.

Over the next few years, English settlers continued to make the journey to Plymouth Colony. When they arrived, they often found that earlier settlers had taken the best farmland. The new arrivals needed to look elsewhere for good land on which to build. Other people wanted to escape the strict Puritan lifestyle in Plymouth and the rest of the Massachusetts Bay Colony. Before long, people began exploring the cape as a place to make homes.

## THE TOWN OF MASHPEE

The town of Mashpee on Cape Cod has a unique history. Mashpee is the only cape town that was legally the property of the natives of the area. In 1660, settler Richard Bourne petitioned the Massachusetts Bay Colony to set aside fifty acres of land for the Native Americans who were being displaced by the English. Today, Mashpee is the home of the Wampanoag nation.

## MAYFLOWER COMPACT

While anchored in Provincetown Harbor, the Pilgrims drew up a document called the Mayflower Compact. The compact stated that all who lived in Plymouth Colony would agree to obey the government that the Pilgrims would establish. Nearly all the men on board signed the compact.

The first three permanent cape towns were founded in 1639. The last town to be settled there was Provincetown, at the very tip of the cape, in 1727. In the early colonial days, the towns were quite isolated from one another. To keep in touch, packet boats sailed from settlement to settlement, bringing crops, fish, merchandise, and messages. Before long, each new town had its own packet boat.

*In 1620, the Mayflower Compact established the basis for written laws among the settlers in the New World.*

# Commerce on the Cape

The first settlers on the cape were farmers who grew corn and other crops that they needed to survive. The sandy soil of the cape made farming a difficult endeavor. In addition to corn, farmers managed to grow beans, grain, strawberries, and squash, including pumpkins. Many of the farmers also raised cattle and sheep, using wool from the sheep to make clothing. In the 1800s, cranberry harvesting became an important industry on the cape. For a time, Cape Cod was the top producer of cranberries in the world.

Like other colonists along the Atlantic coast, early Cape Cod residents turned to the sea to make a living. Fishermen caught cod, herring, haddock, oysters, clams, lobsters, and scallops in the waters around the cape. In the days before refrigeration, cod and other fish were dried and salted to preserve them before shipping. In the early 1900s, the fish were packed in ice and then shipped. Fishing is still an important industry in Cape Cod.

In the 1600s, Cape Cod pioneered what would become its most lucrative industry yet: whaling. Early settlers used dead whales that washed up on their shores, boiling down the blubber to make oil. Later, settlers in small boats drove whales onto the beach, stranding them. By the late 1600s, Cape Cod whalers, equipped with harpoons, were hunting the whales right off the coast.

## SANDWICH GLASS

In 1824, Deming Jarvis founded the Boston and Sandwich Glass Company in the town of Sandwich on Cape Cod. Jarvis chose Sandwich because it had an abundant supply of sand, a key element in making glass. Unfortunately, Sandwich's sand was not the right type for glassmaking. Jarvis had to have sand shipped to the cape from New Jersey and Florida. Over the next six decades, the Sandwich glass factory made many beautiful glass pieces, including paperweights, vases, and candlesticks. Today, the glass is highly prized by antique collectors.

The Cape Cod whalers quickly gained a reputation as experts of the industry. They were so effective, in fact, that soon the waters around the cape were empty of whales. The Cape Cod whalers began to sail to the South Pacific and the Arctic in search of their quarry. During the heyday of whaling in the 1800s, New Bedford, Nantucket, and Provincetown were the most important whaling ports.

Other businesses on Cape Cod included shipbuilders, tanneries, saltworks, iron foundries, and glassmakers. But toward the end of the 1800s, many of the cape's once thriving industries began to fail as other areas of the country began providing the same services for less money. Many people left the cape to seek employment elsewhere.

## TESTING THE RADIO

In 1902, Guglielmo Marconi built four steel towers in Wellfleet on the Cape. Months later, the first wireless telegraph message from the United States was transmitted by radio from President Theodore Roosevelt in Wellfleet to King Edward VII in Cornwall, England. Over the next decade, the radio would revolutionize communication throughout the world.

*Guglielmo Marconi is seen testing his radio in 1901. Early radios were called "wireless telegraphs" because they transmitted only dots and dashes in Morse code instead of voices.*

# A Dangerous Passage

To travel between Boston and New York, ships were forced to navigate along the cape's treacherous eastern shore. As more and more ships sailed between the two important ports, the cape waters acquired a sinister reputation. Over the years, more than 3,000 ships have sunk or run aground in the area.

For people along the coast, the shipwrecks were an opportunity to make money. Shore residents collected the goods that floated to shore, selling them for a profit to whoever would buy. This activity gave rise to the myth of "mooncussers," people who would wave lanterns on the shore on moonless nights, trying to lure passing ships to their doom on the shoals.

Eventually, enterprising people in Cape Cod turned the scavenging into business. Professional salvagers offered their services to ship owners. Armed with axes and crowbars, the salvagers rescued as much of a ship's cargo as they could before the ship sank or broke apart.

Beginning in the late 1700s, Cape Cod officials looked for ways to reduce the danger to ships in the area. In 1797, the first lighthouse along the cape was built in Truro. Later, at least twenty more lighthouses were built to guide sailors safely around the cape. Seven of the lights are still in operation.

## CAPE COD CANAL

Traveling between Boston and New York became quicker and less dangerous in 1914, when the Cape Cod Canal opened. The canal cuts through the bottom of the cape, creating a pathway from Cape Cod Bay to Buzzards Bay. It is 17 miles (27.2 kilometers) long and 540 feet wide (162 meters) at its widest point. The canal cuts the distance between the two big ports by 75 miles (120 kilometers).

# A Summer Destination

In the early 1900s, Cape Cod turned to tourism as a way to keep the economy healthy. Arriving by steamship, and later by train, visitors from New York, Boston, and other New England cities soon discovered the wildness and beauty of the cape. By the 1940s, the cape was the top tourist destination in the Northeast.

*Cape Cod's many natural harbors attract sailors today, just as they did in past centuries. When hurricane warning flags go up, sailors seek the safety of these calmer waters.*

Today, tourism is the cape's biggest industry. Every year, people come from around the world to enjoy fishing, swimming, boating, and sunbathing on the cape. Inns, motels, restaurants, and gift shops are a common sight in most cape towns. During the summertime, the cape population nearly triples.

One popular attraction is the Cape Cod National Seashore. The seashore is a protected area that covers nearly 44,000 acres (17,600 hectares) on the cape's northeastern coast. Founded in 1961, the area includes sand dunes, beaches, freshwater ponds, and nature trails.

# Chesapeake Bay

**5**

hesapeake Bay is a large inlet of water in eastern Maryland and eastern Virginia. The two states share the bay, with Maryland controlling the waters from the Potomac River north. The bay is about 200 miles (320 kilometers) long and ranges from 3 to 25 miles (4.8 to 40 kilometers) in width. The waters of the bay are very shallow, averaging only 24 feet (7.2 meters) in depth.

Chesapeake Bay is the largest natural estuary in the United States. An *estuary* is a body of water in which saltwater from the ocean mixes with freshwater from a river. The Atlantic Ocean at the bottom of the bay provides the saltwater; the hundreds of rivers and streams that empty into the bay provide the fresh. Two of the largest freshwater rivers flowing into the bay are the Susquehanna and the Potomac.

The bay took on its present form about 10,000 years ago, at the end of the last Ice Age. As temperatures began to warm, glaciers in the Northeast melted. Ocean levels rose and floodwaters filled the bay.

## ESTUARIES IN THE UNITED STATES

| Estuary | Location | Length | Width |
|---|---|---|---|
| Chesapeake Bay | Maryland and Virginia | 200 miles (320 kilometers) | 3 to 25 miles (4.8 to 40 kilometers) |
| San Francisco Bay | California | 50 miles (80 kilometers) | 3 to 12 miles (4.8 to 19.2 kilometers) |
| Galveston Bay | Texas | 30 miles (48 kilometers) | 17 miles (27.2 kilometers) |
| Long Island Sound | New York and Connecticut | 110 miles (176 kilometers) | 20 miles (32 kilometers) |
| Tampa Bay | Florida | 25 miles (40 kilometers) | 5 to 7 miles (8 to 11.2 kilometers) |

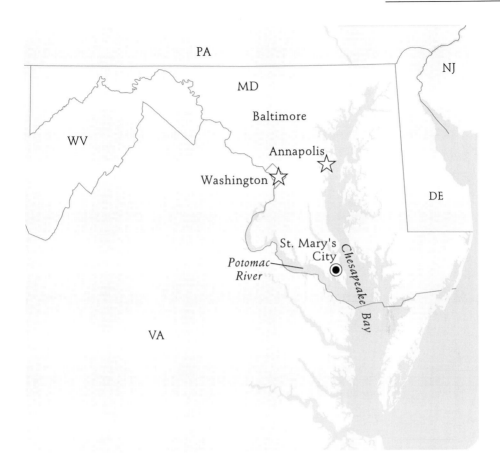

# Settlement
## on the Chesapeake

As in other areas of the Northeast, Native American tribes were the first people to settle in the Chesapeake Bay area. Ten thousand years ago, groups of the earliest Northeast natives hunted along the bay's banks. Later, such tribes as the Susquehannock, Potomac, and Nanticoke settled in the area. They began growing crops of beans, squash, corn, and tobacco. The native tribes also fished and took oysters and other shellfish from the bay waters.

In the 1500s, the first Europeans ventured into the bay. These early adventurers, both French and Spanish, did not stay to settle the area. In 1608, Englishman John Smith explored and mapped the bay. Smith had arrived in America a year earlier with a group of English settlers who founded Jamestown on the Virginia side of the bay.

**THE GREAT SHELLFISH BAY**

The word *Chesapeake* comes from an Algonquian term, *Chesepioc*, meaning "great shellfish bay." In the 1500s, the first Spanish explorers called the bay *La Bahia de la Madre de Dios*, "the Bay of the Mother of God."

The first settlement in the northeast section of the Chesapeake was St. Mary's City, Maryland. The English settlers were the first people to challenge Virginia's claim to the entire Chesapeake Bay area. More people arriving in the area founded other settlements. Two important Chesapeake towns are Annapolis (settled in 1695) and Baltimore (settled in 1729). By 1775, there were about 700,000 people in the Chesapeake Bay area.

**THE ARK AND THE DOVE**

On March 25, 1634, the ships *Ark* and *Dove*, bearing passengers from England, arrived in the territory called Maryland. The 128 settlers, all Catholic, knew that they would not be welcomed by the Protestants in the Virginia territory. Instead, they settled across the bay, on St. Clement's Island, at the mouth of the Potomac River. After receiving permission to remain there from the Piscataway natives, the settlers founded St. Mary's City. St. Mary's would serve as Maryland's capital for more than sixty years. By 1720, however, the town had completely disappeared.

*opposite: The few remaining skipjacks dredge for oysters in Chesapeake Bay in 1999. In 1910, more than 2,000 of these vessels worked the bay. Today, only about ten remain.*

# Commerce around Chesapeake Bay

Over the years, people who lived in the Chesapeake area turned to a number of different industries, nearly all of them supported by the bay waters. Farming, trading, fishing, and shipbuilding all contributed greatly to the region's economy. In recent years, tourism has also played a large part in the growth and health of the bay area.

## Tobacco Farming

The earliest settlers took advantage of the fertile land along the shore. They planted cotton, flax, wheat, corn, and other vegetables. One of the most important crops grown in the northern Chesapeake area was tobacco.

Tobacco farmers quickly learned that they needed many workers to tend the crops and clear new fields for planting. The need for workers in the bay area led directly to the slave trade in America. By 1775, one-third of the people in the Chesapeake Bay area, including Virginia and Maryland, were Africans, most of them slaves. In addition to slave labor, farmers used indentured servants to work the fields. Indentured servants were people who agreed to work for a certain amount of time in order to pay for their passage from Europe to America.

## Fishing

Another important industry in the Chesapeake area was fishing. Fishermen in the area took bass, shad, trout, and pickerel from bay waters, as well as clams, crabs, and other shellfish. One of the largest segments of the fishing industry was oysters.

After the Civil War (1861–1865), the demand for Chesapeake Bay oysters skyrocketed. Fishermen took the oysters from the bay and sent them to packing plants along the shore. After the oysters were packed into cans or bottles, they were sent all over the United States by train or ship. In the late 1870s, this booming business led to the "Oyster Wars" between Virginia and Maryland fishermen. To stop the wars, officials from Virginia and Maryland met and more clearly defined each state's claim to the bay.

Today, oysters and other fish are still a big part of the Chesapeake's economy. About 500 million pounds (225 million kilograms) of seafood come out of the bay each year.

*Tall ships sail on Chesapeake Bay, just as they did hundreds of years ago. These proud vessels are headed for the 1995 Great Chesapeake Bay Schooner Race from Baltimore, Maryland, to Norfolk, Virginia.*

## DEFENCE OF FORT M'HENRY.

The annexed song was composed under the following circumstances—A gentleman had left Baltimore, in a flag of truce for the purpose of getting released from the British fleet, a friend of his who had been captured at Marlborough.—He went as far as the mouth of the Patuxent, and was not permitted to return lest the intended attack on Baltimore should be disclosed. He was therefore brought up the Bay to the mouth of the Patapsco, where the flag vessel was kept under the guns of a frigate, and he was compelled to witness the bombardment of Fort M'Henry, which the Admiral had boasted that he would carry in a few hours, and that the city must fall. He watched the flag at the Fort through the whole day with an anxiety that can be better felt than described, until the night prevented him from seeing it. In the night he watched the Bomb Shells, and at early dawn his eye was again greeted by the proudly waving flag of his country.

*Tune—*ANACREON IN HEAVEN.

O ! say can you see by the dawn's early light,
    What so proudly we hailed at the twilight's last gleaming,
Whose broad stripes and bright stars through the perilous fight,
    O'er the ramparts we watch'd, were so gallantly streaming?
And the Rockets' red glare, the Bombs bursting in air,
Gave proof through the night that our Flag was still there;
    O ! say does that star-spangled Banner yet wave,
    O'er the Land of the free, and the home of the brave?

On the shore dimly seen through the mists of the deep,
    Where the foe's haughty host in dread silence reposes,
What is that which the breeze, o'er the towering steep,
    As it fitfully blows, half conceals, half discloses?
Now it catches the gleam of the morning's first beam,
In full glory reflected now shines in the stream,
    'Tis the star spangled banner, O! long may it wave
    O'er the lard of the free and the home of the brave.

And where is that band who so vauntingly swore
    That the havoc of war and the battle's confusion,
A home and a country, shall leave us no more?
    Their blood has washed out their foul footsteps pollution.
No refuge could save the hireling and slave,
From the terror of flight or the gloom of the grave,
    And the star-spangled banner in triumph doth wave,
    O'er the Land of the Free, and the Home of the Brave.

O! thus be it ever when freemen shall stand,
    Between their lov'd home, and the war's desolation,
Blest with vict'ry and peace, may the Heav'n rescued land,
    Praise the Power that hath made and preserv'd us a nation!
Then conquer we must, when our cause it is just,
And this be our motto—" In God is our Trust;"
    And the star-spangled Banner in triumph shall wave,
    O'er the Land of the Free, and the Home of the Brave.

## "THE STAR SPANGLED BANNER"

In September 1814, lawyer and poet Francis Scott Key watched the Battle of Fort McHenry from a boat in Baltimore Harbor. The battle between the British and the Americans for this Maryland fort stretched on into the night. In the morning, the U.S. flag was still flying from the fort's ramparts. Inspired, Key penned the words to the song that became our national anthem, "The Star Spangled Banner."

# War and the Chesapeake

During the American Revolution (1775–1783), the Chesapeake area suffered greatly. From 1776 to 1779, the British blockaded the bay, bringing hardship to many Maryland towns. Only British ships bearing supplies for British troops were allowed into the bay.

The bay also helped bring an end to the war. In 1781, the French fleet, on behalf of the American colonists, barricaded the bay. British troops could no longer receive supplies, nor could they retreat by sea. The British were soon forced to surrender. In 1783, the Treaty of Paris, which ended the war, was signed in Annapolis, Maryland's capital.

**A NEW CAPITAL FOR AMERICA**

In 1791, Maryland and Virginia donated land on the Potomac and Anacostia Rivers to be the site of our nation's new capital. First called the District of Columbia, the city was renamed Washington in 1799, after our first president's death.

The War of 1812 (1812–1815) caused further hardships for those who lived near the Chesapeake Bay. The British set up their base of operations on Tangier Island in the Virginia section of the bay. As a result, the bay area saw plenty of naval action during the war. In 1814, the British entered the bay and sailed up the Potomac River. They attacked Washington, D.C., the nation's new capital, burning its public buildings to the ground. The British then moved on to Baltimore and unsuccessfully attempted to capture Fort McHenry.

In 1861, the Civil War split the nation in two. In the years before the war, the issues of slavery and states' rights had caused controversy between North and South. People in Maryland were divided, as well. Although Maryland was a slave-holding state, the Underground Railroad thrived there. The Underground Railroad was a network of antislavery Americans who helped slaves travel to the North, where they could live in freedom.

## HARRIET TUBMAN AND THE UNDERGROUND RAILROAD

Harriet Tubman was born on a Chesapeake plantation around 1820. In 1849, she fled to freedom in Philadelphia, Pennsylvania. Before the Civil War, she became the most famous "conductor" of the Underground Railroad. Tubman made nineteen trips into slave territory to lead about 300 slaves to freedom. She died in 1913.

*In addition to helping other slaves escape, Harriet Tubman nursed Union troops during the Civil War (1861–1865) and went on spying missions for the Union army. It is no wonder she is known as "the Moses of Her People."*

When the war began, Maryland chose to remain in the Union, but because of its shared border with Virginia, a Confederate state, many people's sympathies were with the South. About 22,000 men from Maryland fought for the Confederacy. In the Chesapeake region, the war turned neighbor against neighbor, father against brother.

# The Chesapeake Today

Over the years, the Chesapeake has become more accessible to people in surrounding areas. Beginning in the late nineteenth century, trains and steamships helped the area draw an ever increasing number of tourists. Today, people still come from all over to enjoy the boating, fishing, and natural beauty that can be found only in the bay.

The Chesapeake is a highly populated region. Many people have moved to the western shore area. Consequently, the area is highly developed. On the eastern shore, fishing, farming, and other industries continue to thrive.

The bay's popularity has had some negative side effects. Farming, fishing, and development have all taken a toll. Chemicals and air pollution have made the Chesapeake's water less healthy. Nutrients from crop fertilizers that run into the bay have caused overgrowths of algae. These factors, as well as disease caused by parasites and overfishing, have reduced oyster and fish populations.

In the early 1970s, people in the area realized that the Chesapeake Bay had reached a crisis point. Citizens knew that something must be done to save the bay. In 1972, the Clean Water Act was a first step in the right direction. Then in 1983, Virginia, Maryland, Pennsylvania, and the Environmental Protection Agency (EPA) signed the Chesapeake Bay Agreement. Under the agreement, the states and the agency work together to monitor and protect the bay.

Thanks to these and other efforts, the Chesapeake Bay is on the road to recovery. Chemical bans, fishing guidelines, and caring citizens are helping the waters of the bay become healthier than they have been since the 1970s. Oyster and fish populations are beginning to make a comeback in the bay, too.

# Connecticut River

**6**

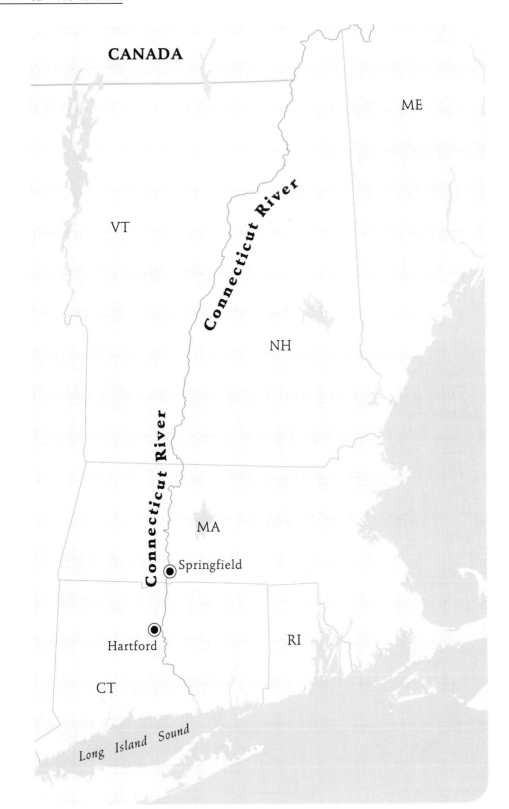

Τhe Connecticut River is the longest river in New England. It winds 410 miles (656 kilometers) through four New England states: Vermont, New Hampshire, Massachusetts, and Connecticut. Because of its historic importance to the growth and development of the area, the Connecticut has been called the Mississippi (River) of New England.

The source of the Connecticut is in the Fourth Connecticut Lake, a small body of water in northern New Hampshire near the Canadian border. As the river flows south toward the Atlantic Ocean, it marks the boundary between New Hampshire and Vermont. It passes through central Massachusetts and into Connecticut. At Old Saybrook, Connecticut, the river empties into the Atlantic Ocean. Along its course, the Connecticut drains a watershed area of more than 11,000 square miles (26,800 square kilometers).

The scenery along much of the northern Connecticut River is wild and beautiful, with rapids,

## COMPARING THE CONNECTICUT

The Connecticut River is the longest in New England. Here's how it compares to some other well-known rivers.

| River | Length |
| --- | --- |
| Connecticut | 410 miles (656 kilometers) |
| Hudson | 315 miles (504 kilometers) |
| Delaware | 400 miles (640 kilometers) |
| Mississippi | 2,348 miles (3,757 kilometers) |
| Missouri | 2,714 miles (4,342 kilometers) |

waterfalls, and gorges. Farther south, the mark of civilization becomes more apparent. Many dairy farms and fields of crops are located in the valley. Nearly a hundred towns are found along the river's edge. In fact, some of the area's most important industrial cities are located on the banks of the Connecticut. More than 2 million people make their homes in the Connecticut River valley.

# The River's History

About 20,000 years ago, thick glaciers covered the Connecticut valley. As the glaciers retreated 12,000 years ago, they carved out the Connecticut River. A thousand years after the last glaciers retreated from the valley, Native Americans began to settle in the area. The earliest groups hunted. Later groups soon learned that the land by the river was fertile and good for farming, especially after the spring floodwaters receded. They planted such crops as corn, pumpkins, squash, and beans. They also fished in the river and dug for clams and mussels.

Before Europeans arrived in the area, there were thousands of native people living along the Connecticut River. These tribes included the Podunk, Nipmuck, Mohegan, Pequot, and Niantic. Today, few traces of these native tribes can be found. One exception is rock carvings, called *petroglyphs*, left behind by the Pennacooks (PEN-eh-kuk) in Vermont.

## NATIVE TERMINOLOGY

The word *Connecticut* comes from the Native American term *Quoneh-ta-cut* or *Quinni-tukq-ut*, which means "long tidal river." The Connecticut colony took its name from the river that was at the center of its earliest history.

# The First Europeans

The first European to venture up the Connecticut River was Dutch sea captain Adriaen Block in 1614. Block, looking for sites to build trading posts, sailed his ship the *Onrust* (*Restless*) 60 miles (96 kilometers) up the river.

Although the Dutch chose not to colonize the area, they did establish trading posts with the native people they met. In 1624, they set up a trading post at the mouth of the Connecticut River. Although this first post didn't last long, the Dutch tried again in 1633. They bought land near what is now Hartford from the Pequot tribe and built a fort and trading post called the House of Hope.

## BLOCK ISLAND

The only landmark to bear the name of Dutch explorer Adriaen Block is Block Island, a small island in the Atlantic Ocean off the coast of Rhode Island. Block discovered the island in 1614 during his expedition up the Connecticut River. The island, first settled in 1661, is a popular tourist destination.

At first, English settlers in the Massachusetts colony had little interest in the Connecticut River valley. When the coastline in Massachusetts became more crowded and new arrivals from England had less available land to choose from, settlers began to look more carefully at the fertile Connecticut valley.

In 1633, settlers from Plymouth Colony set up a trading post just north of the House of Hope. Although the Dutch tried to scare the English settlers away, they were unsuccessful. In the next two years, English settlers founded the towns of Wethersfield and Hartford. Five years later, leaders from the area adopted a constitution that established the Connecticut colony. By 1654, the Dutch had given up all their rights to land along the river to the English.

Eventually, settlers began to choose sites further north up the river. Springfield, the first Massachusetts settlement along the river, was founded in 1636. At the time, it was the northernmost trading post on the river. Within a few decades, people had settled along the entire length of the Connecticut in Massachusetts. This area came to be known as the Pioneer Valley.

## CONNECTICUT RIVER WITCH HUNTS

Forty-five years before the Salem witch trials, settlers in Hartford, Connecticut, were accusing people of being witches. On May 26, 1647, Hartford became the first town in the colonies to execute anyone for witchcraft. The unfortunate victim was a widow named Alice Young. Over the next twenty-three years, eleven people in the Connecticut River valley were tried, sentenced, and killed for being witches.

It wasn't until much later that settlers began living along the river in what is now New Hampshire and Vermont. The first Vermont settlement was founded in 1724, when the English built Fort Dummer, on the site of what is now Brattleboro, to protect the area from the French. In 1734, the first permanent New Hampshire town along the Connecticut was founded in what is now Charlestown, New Hampshire.

# Trouble along the Connecticut

As colonists moved into the Connecticut River valley, they displaced the Native American tribes who had lived there for so long. The settlers wanted the best, most fertile land for their crops. Most of these sites had long been farmed by area tribes. The Connecticut River valley became the site of many raids, as some Native American groups fought to protect their land from the settlers.

The first serious conflict in New England between native tribes and settlers was known as the Pequot War (1637). It began when a group of Pequots attacked some English settlers and traders. The Pequots, a fierce group feared by many tribes in the area, felt that the settlers were encroaching on Pequot land.

The Connecticut colony declared war on the Pequots. In May 1637, soldiers and volunteers attacked a Pequot settlement, killing about 600 men, women, and children. Those who were not killed were sold into slavery, and the Pequot tribe was nearly wiped out in Connecticut.

*The Pequot War (1637) between British colonists and the Pequots almost destroyed this Native American tribe. Today, the Pequots have regained some of their native lands in eastern Connecticut.*

## King Philip's War

Relations between the native tribes and the colonists remained quiet for nearly forty years. Then in 1675, the bloodiest, most devastating war in New England's history began. King Philip's War was led by Metacom, the leader of the Wampanoag (wahm-puh-NO-uck) people. Metacom, called King Philip by the colonists, was the son of Massasoit. Massasoit, ironically, was the Wampanoag chief who had helped the Pilgrims survive their first winter in Plymouth.

Metacom did not share his father's friendly feelings toward the settlers. Since the English had first arrived in 1620, the tribes of the area had suffered. Many Native Americans had been wiped out by such European diseases as smallpox and yellow fever. Many more had lost their land to the new arrivals.

King Philip's War (1675–1676) began outside of the Connecticut valley when three Wampanoags were executed in Massachusetts for the murder of another native. The furious Wampanoags began attacking settlers in eastern Massachusetts and Rhode Island. Soon Metacom and his warriors turned their attention to the Connecticut River valley. Here, the newly formed settlements were poorly defended and easier to attack.

Other tribes that had been pushed off their land soon joined the Wampanoags in their raids. At first, the warriors attacked small groups of farmers working out in the fields. Then they began to attack whole towns, killing or capturing the citizens and burning the towns to the ground. During the war, fifty-two settlements were attacked; up to thirteen towns were destroyed. Perhaps as many as 1,000 colonists were killed.

There were bloody acts of violence on both sides. Colonists, for example, wiped out hundreds of Narragansetts, mostly women and children, at their winter camp in Rhode Island. Called the Great Swamp Massacre, the attack on the tribe was meant to keep them out of the war. After the massacre, however, surviving Narragansetts joined the warring tribes.

As the war continued, the tribes became hungry and weak. Because of the fighting, they had been unable to plant crops to sustain them through the long winter. The war ended in 1676 when Metacom was killed.

Hundreds of colonists had suffered, but the native tribes had taken the worst of it. After King Philip's War, most tribes in the area were reduced to ruins. There would be no more native resistance to European settlement of the Connecticut River valley.

## THE END OF METACOM

After Metacom's death, his head was chopped off and displayed in Plymouth for twenty years. His wife and son, along with about 500 other hostile natives, were sold into slavery in the West Indies.

## MARY ROWLANDSON

In February 1676, the small town of Lancaster, Massachusetts, was attacked by a band of Native Americans. The town was destroyed, and thirteen people were killed. Mary Rowlandson was one of twenty-four townspeople taken hostage. Over the next three months, she and the others were forced to march through Vermont and New Hampshire. Rowlandson was finally released in May. In 1682, she published an account of her experience, called *A Narrative of the Captivity and Removes of Mrs. Mary Rowlandson*.

# The Economy of the Connecticut

Because of the rich floodplains around the Connecticut River's banks, the area quickly became a center for farming in colonial New England. Farmers grew grain, corn, rye, oats, barley, and many other crops, earning the Connecticut River valley the nickname "breadbasket of New England."

Another important crop was tobacco. In 1801, a Connecticut woman on a South Windsor farm rolled the first U.S. cigars. Today, farmers along the river's banks still grow tobacco. They also grow potatoes,

*The Holyoke Dam harnesses the power of the Connecticut River. Holyoke, Massachusetts was built around a system of canals and dams that were begun in 1847.*

onions, asparagus, apples, strawberries, and other vegetables in the fertile soil. Dairy farming is also an important industry in the area.

In addition to fertilizing the farmland, the waters of the Connecticut River also provided the power necessary to run sawmills and gristmills in colonial times. Today, dams on the river provide energy to power plants, as well as pulp and paper mills.

# Shipping and Other Industries

Over the years, one of the most important roles of the Connecticut River has been as a major transportation route through central New England to the sea. The native tribes were the first people to use the river to get from one place to another. When colonists began settling along the river in the mid-1600s, the native peoples transported furs from up north to the settlers' trading posts farther down the river.

Shipbuilding and shipping became important industries along the Connecticut in the 1700s. The first shipbuilding operation in the region was started in 1649 in Wethersfield, Connecticut. Over the years, the Connecticut River was home to more than forty shipyards that built boats of every kind, including schooners, sloops, clipper ships, and whalers.

In the late 1600s, Connecticut ports became centers for trade with the West Indies. The colonists shipped wheat, potatoes, cheese, and livestock in return for sugar, rum, and molasses. Some ship owners also began to transport slaves from Africa

## CROSSING THE CONNECTICUT

Ferries were one of the first ways that people got from one bank of the Connecticut to the other. The first ferries were canoes, followed by flatboats. These large, flat-bottomed boats were sometimes propelled by sails, sometimes by oars. In some spots, the flatboats were pulled from one bank to the other along ropes strung across the river.

The very first ferry on the Connecticut River began operating in 1641 in Windsor, Connecticut. A ferry in Connecticut between Rocky Hill and Glastonbury, which opened in 1655, is still operating today. It is the oldest continuously operating ferry on the river—and possibly in the nation.

back to the New England colonies. Slavery continued to be a part of life in the colonies. In Connecticut, there were more than 6,000 black slaves in 1774, the year the state stopped importing slaves.

In the nineteenth century, with the advent of the Industrial Revolution, new businesses sprang up along the river. River access made it easier for these companies to ship their products to market. Products that have been built on the banks of the river include firearms, printing presses, ivory piano keys, beer, and even aircraft engines.

Another innovation changed life on the Connecticut in the early nineteenth century: the steamboat. In 1813, the first commercial steamboat plied the waters of the Connecticut, carrying passengers from Middletown to Hartford. In 1825, steamboats began regular runs between Hartford and New York City, two thriving port cities. The age of the steamboat didn't last long, however. In the late 1860s, the first railroad south of Hartford marked the beginning of the end of steamboats on the Connecticut.

## CONNECTICUT RIVER FIRSTS

- The oldest continuously published newspaper in the United States, *The Hartford Courant*, was published in Hartford, Connecticut, beginning in 1764. The *Courant* is still published today.

- The *American Turtle*, the first submarine used in warfare, was built in Old Saybrook, Connecticut, in 1775.

- The first U.S. warship, the *Oliver Cromwell*, was built in Essex, Connecticut, in 1776.

- What may have been the first canal in the United States was built in 1795 in South Hadley, Massachusetts.

- In 1891, James Naismith invented the game of basketball in Springfield, Massachusetts.

# Today

Throughout the Connecticut's history, some of the same forces that helped cities and towns thrive around the river also harmed the river itself. Over the years, dumping, damming, sewage overflows, powerboats, and riverside development made the Connecticut one of the most polluted rivers in the nation.

As the Connecticut got dirtier, people began to worry about preserving it. In 1972, first steps were taken to clean up the river: The Clean Water Act regulated all dumping in the river. Since then, the health of the Connecticut River has greatly improved. On July 30, 1998, the Connecticut was named one of the first fourteen American Heritage Rivers. As an

*The Riverfront redevelopment project is reclaiming the banks of the Connecticut River in Hartford, Connecticut. Years of neglect and pollution are being reversed along this great American river.*

American Heritage River, the Connecticut River will receive more attention from federal agencies that can help preserve and maintain it.

# Delaware River

**7**

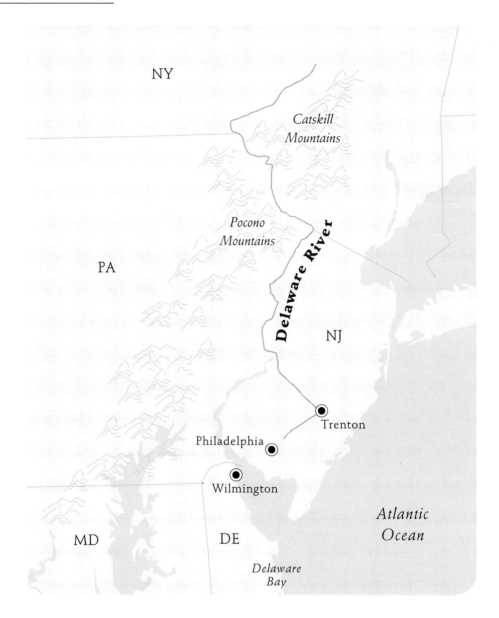

T he Delaware River is one of the most
important rivers in the Northeast. Over the
centuries, the river has played a key part in
the nation's history. Since the 1600s, it has
served as an important commercial waterway.

The Delaware River has its source in the Catskill
Mountains in New York. It begins as two branches

that join together in Hancock, New York. The river winds nearly 400 miles (640 kilometers) through four Northeast states. It serves as the boundary between Pennsylvania and New York, between Pennsylvania and New Jersey, and between Delaware and New Jersey. It empties into Delaware Bay.

Many heavily populated and important commercial areas are located along the lower part of the Delaware River. Large cities include Trenton, New Jersey; Philadelphia, Pennsylvania; and Wilmington, Delaware. These cities grew near the river because residents could use the water supplied by the river and travel easily by boat. The Delaware River is a chief source of fresh water for New York City and other metropolitan areas.

Important tributaries, rivers that run into the Delaware, include the Schuylkill and Lehigh Rivers. The Delaware Water Gap, a 2-mile (3.2-kilometer) long gorge (a deep, narrow canyon) in the Kittatinny Mountains, is a well-known scenic attraction. It was named a national recreation area in 1965.

# Settlement

The first people to live near the Delaware River were the ancestors of later Native American tribes. These early Americans arrived about 10,000 years ago. They were nomadic groups that hunted and foraged along the river and in the surrounding forests.

Before Europeans arrived, an important tribe in the area was the *Lenni Lenape* (len-NAH-pay). The name Lenni Lenape means "the original people" or "the real men." Later, English explorers would call the tribe the "Delaware," for the river they lived near. Beginning in the 1600s, the Susquehannock people also moved into the region.

*This woodcut depicts the purchase of Manhattan Island from the Lenape by Peter Minuit in 1626. It is believed he paid the equivalent of $24 in trade goods.*

# The Arrival of Europeans

In the early 1600s, Dutch explorers began trading with the Lenape people along the Delaware River. The river area was rich in beaver and other animals, and the Dutch exchanged trinkets and tools for animal furs. The Dutch claimed the area as part of New Netherland, the Dutch colony in the New World. It stretched from the Hudson River in New York down the coast to Delaware Bay.

The Dutch explored the river valley but did not establish any permanent settlements there. The first permanent European settlement in the area was founded by the Swedish in 1638, when Peter Minuit sailed the *Kalmar Nyckel* (Key of Kalmar) and the *Fogel Grip* (Flying Griffin) into Delaware Bay. Minuit had once been the leader of New Netherland. Now working for Sweden's Queen Christina, Minuit claimed the Delaware area and named it New Sweden.

Under Minuit's command, Swedish and Finnish settlers built Fort Christina. Today, Wilmington, Delaware, is located where Fort Christina stood. In 1643, the Swedish settlers decided to move further up the river for safety. The new capital of New Sweden was established on Tinicum Island near what is now Philadelphia. Called New Gothenburg, it was the first permanent European settlement in Pennsylvania.

When the Swedish settlers arrived in 1638, they blocked the Dutch access to the river. Of course, the Dutch were not happy with this new situation. In 1655, after a few years of bickering with the Swedes, the Dutch claimed that the entire area was theirs. Under command of Peter Stuyvesant, New Netherland's governor, the Dutch sailed up the Delaware and easily took control of the area. New Sweden had survived in the New World for just seventeen years.

## RIVER NAMES

In 1610, English explorers named the river after Sir Thomas West, Baron De La Warr. West was the first governor of the Virginia Territory. Over the centuries, however, the Delaware River has had many other names.

- Lenape Wihittuck
- Zuydt, or South, River
- Prince Hendrick River
- Charles River
- New Sweden Stream

# The English Take Over

Dutch rule of the Delaware River area would be even shorter than that of the Swedes. Within ten years, the English decided that they wanted control of the entire East Coast. In 1664, King Charles II of England awarded New England, New Jersey, and New York—which included the entire New Netherland territory—to his brother James, the Duke of York. King Charles ordered James to head to America and take control of his new property.

In September 1664, the English fleet sailed into New York Bay and demanded that the Dutch hand over New Netherland. The Dutch quietly surrendered all of their territory in the New World, including the land along the Delaware River.

By 1680, about 2,000 people were living in the Delaware River region. Settlers included Swedish, Finnish, Dutch, and English colonists. In 1681, however, an event took place that would open up the area to massive settlement. That year, King Charles II granted William Penn a 48,000-acre (19,200-hectare) chunk of land in America. The King named Penn's new territory "Pennsylvania."

Penn had more in mind than just founding his own colony. Penn was a Quaker, and he wanted his new territory to be a "holy experiment." A Quaker is a member of a religious group which is also known as the Society of Friends. Quakers believe in simple prayer services and nonviolence, among other things. Penn envisioned a place where people of all religions could live together in peace. He even began drawing up the plans for a city in this new land. He named the city Philadelphia, which means "city of brotherly love."

## SWEDISH LOG HOMES

The log home was an innovation brought to America by Swedish and Finnish settlers along the Delaware River. The Scandinavian settlers built their homes out of long logs. No nails were needed: The logs were fitted together by notches carved out with an ax. Log homes became the standard home for early American pioneers.

In 1682, Penn and a group of English Quakers boarded the *Welcome* and sailed for Pennsylvania. Soon, hundreds of people from countries all across Europe had made their way to Pennsylvania. These early settlers came from England, Ireland, Wales, Scotland, Germany, the Netherlands, and Switzerland.

Philadelphia, located on the Delaware and Schuylkill Rivers, offered ships a deep harbor in which to anchor. Its location on the Delaware made it the perfect site for settlement and trade to and from England. As a result, the city thrived and grew rapidly. By 1720, Philadelphia had a population of 10,000 citizens. It was one of the largest cities in the colonies—second only to Boston, Massachusetts.

## PENN AND DELAWARE

From 1667 to 1682, the territory that is now Delaware was controlled by the English as part of New York. In 1682, the King of England allowed William Penn to add the region to Pennsylvania. Delaware became known as the "three lower counties." The colonists of Delaware, however, wanted to govern themselves. They resented being governed by Quaker lawmakers in Philadelphia. So in 1704, the people of Delaware established their own body of lawmakers. More than eighty years later, Delaware became the first state in the United States of America. On December 1, 1787, Delaware's lawmakers accepted the U.S. Constitution.

### • Fast Fact •

New Castle, founded in 1651 by the Dutch as Fort Casimir, was Delaware's first state capital. New Castle lasted as state capital for just one year, from 1776 to 1777. In 1777, the capital was moved to Dover.

# Commerce and Travel

The earliest commerce along the Delaware River was the fur trade. The first trading posts were built by the Dutch West India Company. These early Dutch posts along the Delaware included Fort Nassau, at present-day Gloucester, New Jersey; and Fort Casimir, which is now New Castle, Delaware.

Because of easy access to the Atlantic Ocean from the Delaware, shipping quickly became a major industry in the region. From its earliest beginnings, Philadelphia was one of the most important trading and shipping ports in the colonies. Before the American Revolution (1775–1783), hundreds of Philadelphians worked in shipping-related industries, such as shipbuilding, marketing, sail making, coopering, and blacksmithing. Other important Delaware River ports during colonial times included Wilmington and New Castle, Delaware.

In the 1780s, the Delaware was the site of a historic happening. On August 22, 1787, inventor John Fitch used the river to launch the very first steamboat. Three years later, Fitch began steamboat service between Philadelphia and Burlington, New Jersey. Although Fitch built the first steamboats, he was unable to get financial backing for his project. As a result, Fitch never received the credit or success that he deserved.

In 1829, a canal, or artificial waterway, connecting the Delaware River and Chesapeake Bay was completed. The 19-mile (30.4-kilometer) Chesapeake and Delaware Canal conveniently connected Philadelphia and Baltimore, Maryland. It shortened the trip between the two cities by about 300 miles (480 kilometers), because ships no longer had to sail all the way around the Delmarva Peninsula. Trade between the two important cities skyrocketed.

The coming of the railroads in the late 1830s also increased the region's growth as a major trade center.

With railways to connect the big cities along the Delaware to other urban trade centers in the Northeast, the river cities grew in importance. In 1838, rail lines connected Philadelphia and Wilmington. Sixteen years later, the Pennsylvania Railroad connected Philadelphia to Pittsburgh, an iron and steel center in the western part of Pennsylvania.

During the twentieth century, shipping and shipbuilding continued to be important industries along the Delaware. During World War I (1914–1918), Philadelphia shipyards produced many warships. The city became known as an "arsenal of democracy." An *arsenal* is a building where weapons are made or stored. During World War II (1939–1945), the United States Navy Yard in the city built warships and repaired and serviced other ships for wartime duty.

*The newly constructed battleship USS New Jersey slides into the water at the Philadelphia Navy shipyard on December 7, 1942. This was exactly one year following the Japanese attack on Pearl Harbor.*

Today, the Delaware River continues to be an important commercial river. Many factories and plants line its banks. One of the largest and most famous industrial companies along the Delaware is DuPont Chemicals, located in Wilmington. Founded in 1802, DuPont started as a gunpowder factory. Eleuthére Irenée du Pont de Nemours began the business with a saltpeter mill. The mill used water power from the Brandywine River, a tributary of the Delaware, to manufacture the gunpowder.

# Revolution along the Delaware

The Delaware River area played an important part in American history during the American Revolution. Philadelphia, in particular, was the site of many historic happenings. In September 1774, for example, the First Continental Congress met in Philadelphia. During this meeting, representatives of the thirteen colonies encouraged citizens to take up arms and defend their rights.

The Second Continental Congress was meeting in Philadelphia in June 1775, when war between Great Britain and the colonies began. More than a year later, on July 4, 1776, members of the Second Continental Congress signed the Declaration of Independence. Four days after the document was signed, it was read out loud in public throughout Philadelphia, and bells were rung in celebration.

At the beginning of the war, Philadelphia was the largest city in the colonies. More than 25,000 people made their homes there. After the United States declared its freedom from Great Britain, Philadelphia was quickly chosen as the new nation's capital. It soon became a key target for British troops. In March 1776, British ships blockaded Delaware Bay. This action seriously harmed the shipping industry in the area because ships carrying cargo could not get past the blockade.

*Although George Washington disliked posing for portraits, he was painted many times. Here he is shown before the Battle of Trenton during the American Revolution (1775–1783).*

Many famous battles of the revolution were fought in the Delaware River region. One of the earliest was the Battle of Trenton. Late on Christmas night in 1776, General George Washington crossed the Delaware River from Pennsylvania to Trenton, New Jersey. He surprised the British the next morning and won the battle.

Another important battle was the Battle of Brandywine. This famous battle took place on the Brandywine River, a tributary of the Delaware, in September 1777. After American troops lost the battle, the Continental Congress was forced to flee from Philadelphia. Less than two weeks later, General Washington's troops attempted to take back the city. They were defeated in the Battle of Germantown. However, the British held Philadelphia for less than a year before abandoning it.

When the war was over, Philadelphia played an important role in the formation of the new nation's government. The U.S. Constitution was written and signed in Philadelphia in 1787. The city served as the nation's capital from 1790 to 1800.

*More than 2 million people come to Liberty Bell Pavilion each year to see and touch this symbol of freedom.*

## • Fast Fact •

**The Liberty Bell was shipped from England to Philadelphia in 1752. The first time the bell was rung, it cracked. The bell was recast and hung in Pennsylvania's State House in 1753. After the Declaration of Independence was signed there in 1776, the State House was renamed Independence Hall.**

## FAMOUS PHILADELPHIANS

Philadelphia has been the home of many famous folk. Here are just a few:

- *Benjamin Franklin*: Franklin moved to Philadelphia at the age of seventeen. He quickly became one of the city's most prominent citizens. A printer, inventor, and politician, Franklin helped write the Declaration of Independence and the U.S. Constitution.
- *Betsy Ross*: Betsy Griscom Ross was born in Philadelphia in 1752. Legend has it that Ross designed and created the first American flag.
- *Marian Anderson*: Born in Philadelphia in 1897, Anderson was a classical singer. After being prevented from singing in Constitution Hall because she was African American, Anderson was invited to sing in front of the Lincoln Memorial by First Lady Eleanor Roosevelt.
- *Bill Cosby*: The famous comedian, actor, and writer was born in Philadelphia in 1937.

# Today

Beginning in the early 1700s, pollution began taking a toll along the lower Delaware River. During industrial development in the nineteenth and twentieth centuries, the river and surrounding areas became even more polluted. Factory runoff, sewage, and air pollution all contributed to make the Delaware one of the dirtiest rivers in the nation.

In the 1930s, people in the Delaware Valley area recognized that something had to be done. In 1936, the Interstate Commission on the Delaware Basin (INCODEL) was created. The commission prohibited towns from dumping sewage into the river.

Two decades later, pollution problems still persisted. Fish and other wildlife were unable to survive. In the 1950s, some parts of the river—especially spots near Philadelphia and other big cities—were declared dead. Since 1961, people from the four states through which the Delaware runs have worked hard to help the river. That year, those four states, along with the U.S. government, formed a 100-year partnership to carefully monitor and control how the river is used. Although the water is still not clean enough for swimming, the river is slowly recovering.

# Hudson
# River

**8**

**T**he Hudson River in eastern New York is one of the key waterways in the Northeast. The Hudson begins in Lake Tear of the Clouds, a lake at the top of Mount Marcy, the highest mountain in the Adirondacks. From the lake, the river rambles 315 miles (504 kilometers), through Saratoga Springs, Albany, Troy, Poughkeepsie, and many other New York towns. It passes through the Catskill and Taconic Mountains before emptying into New York Bay.

Over the years, the Hudson has played an important role in New York's—and America's—history.

Lake Tear of the Clouds

Mohawk River

⊙ Albany

NY

Hudson River

New York Bay

## THE PALISADES

The Palisades, near the mouth of the Hudson, are one of the river's most awe-inspiring sights. These sheer cliffs tower between 200 and 540 feet (60 and 162 meters) over the Hudson. Geologists believe that the Palisades were formed at the end of the Triassic Period, more than 200 million years ago.

*The New Jersey side of the Hudson River near New York City is called the Palisades. Palisades are lofty, steep cliffs usually found along the banks of a river.*

It was an avenue for trade and commerce from the earliest colonial days. For this reason, the British tried to control the river during the American Revolution (1775–1783). Later, the Erie Canal made the Hudson an even more vital waterway.

Today, the Hudson is famous for its wild beauty. Tall, towering cliffs called the Palisades are a highlight of the Lower Hudson. The Upper Hudson is marked by many beautiful waterfalls and rapids. In addition, there are a number of historic landmarks along its shores, including the Franklin Delano Roosevelt Library, the home of author Washington Irving, and the United States Military Academy at West Point.

# Hudson History

The Hudson River was formed thousands of years ago by glaciers that carved out a deep valley. As these glaciers melted, the sea level rose, filling what is now New York Bay and the Hudson River with water.

Native American tribes lived in the Hudson River area as early as 10,000 years ago. They found everything they needed in this fertile region. The tribes planted crops along the banks of the river. They hunted for deer, rabbit, and other game in the woodlands, and they fished in the Hudson, catching bass, shad, and mackerel. Tribes that lived along the Hudson included the Lenape, Mahican, Wappinger, and Iroquois.

The first European to sight the Hudson River was Giovanni da Verrazano (gee-oh-VAHN-ee dah ver-rah-ZAHN-oh) in 1524. However, Verrazano did not

## STATE RIVER STATS

The Hudson is the longest river in New York State. Here's a look at some rivers in other states of the Northeast.

| State | River | Length |
|-------|-------|--------|
| New York | Hudson | 315 miles (504 kilometers) |
| Vermont | Otter Creek | 100 miles (160 kilometers) |
| Maine | Penobscot | 350 miles (560 kilometers) |
| Maryland | Potomac | 285 miles (456 kilometers) |
| Massachusetts | Charles | 80 miles (128 kilometers) |

explore further. Eighty-five years later, Henry Hudson became the first European to sail up the river. In the *Half Moon*, Hudson sailed about 150 miles (240 kilometers) upriver to where Albany is located today. Hudson was impressed by what he saw. When he returned to the Netherlands, he recommended that the Dutch claim the river and its surrounding land.

## NAMING A RIVER

Before Europeans settled the area, Native Americans called the river *Muhheakantuck*, or "the waters that are in constant motion." Henry Hudson called it the Great River of the Mountains, but the Dutch renamed it the Mauritius River in honor of a Dutch national hero. When the British took control of the area in 1664, they named it after Henry Hudson, the Englishman who had first explored the area for the Dutch.

*This engraving from 1856 shows Henry Hudson exploring the river that would one day bear his name. Hudson sailed up the river in 1609 on his ship the* Half Moon.

# Hudson Settlements

In 1614, the Dutch built three trading posts in New Netherland, as they called their territory. At these posts along the river, they gave liquor, blankets, and trinkets to local natives in exchange for animal skins, including beaver, fox, mink, and wildcat. Later, the Dutch and other colonists began using wampum, long strands of clam and oyster shell beads that the natives used as money.

**ALBANY, NEW YORK'S CAPITAL**

In 1624, Albany was the site of the first permanent settlement in New York. Because of its status as a center of transportation, Albany was chosen as New York's capital in 1797. It is still the capital of the Empire State.

In 1624, the first permanent European settlers of the Hudson area arrived. Known as Walloons, these settlers were French-speaking Belgians, sponsored by the Dutch. The Walloons founded a settlement near what is now Albany. They called their settlement Beverwyck.

In 1664, four shiploads of British soldiers sailed into what is now New York Harbor. The British wanted control of this lucrative section of America. Defenseless against the British warships, New Amsterdam's governor, Peter Stuyvesant, surrendered. The Dutch had controlled the area for just over forty years.

The British quickly put their mark on the area, changing the names of many settlements. The town of New Amsterdam became New York, and Beverwyck was renamed Albany. The British even renamed the river itself.

At first, settlers chose to remain near the lower end of the Hudson. They feared attacks from the French and native groups to the north. When the British won the French and Indian War (1754–1763), they pushed the French out of the colonies once and for all. After this, settlement in the upper Hudson River area rapidly increased.

As good land became scarcer in Connecticut and Massachusetts, settlers from these colonies made their way to the Hudson. Most of the settlers were farmers, looking for land of their own to till. These "Yankee" transplants founded the towns of Troy and Hudson.

As more people settled along the Hudson, the area's economy thrived. Farming was an important business, as was shipping. All manner of goods went back and forth between New York City and the Hudson River towns. Lumber, livestock, vegetables, fruit, stone, fish, and furs were sent down the river to be sold or traded. Furniture, silver, china, carpeting, and other niceties made their way upstream.

## War Affects the River

During the American Revolution, the importance of the Hudson River became obvious to both the colonists and the British. If the British took control of the Hudson, they would cut New England troops off from the rest of the colonies. The river was also an important route used to transport troops and supplies.

*The Hudson River fort at West Point became the site of the United States Military Academy in 1802.*

At the outbreak of war, the colonists along the Hudson prepared to fight. Many forts up and down the river were heavily fortified. These forts included West Point, Fort Montgomery, Fort Clinton, and Fort Constitution. At one spot on the river, colonists forged a gigantic iron chain that stretched from one bank to another. Each link in the chain was 2 feet (0.6 meter) long and weighed 140 pounds (63 kilograms) or more. The massive chain was meant to prevent British ships from advancing upriver.

During the war, a number of important battles and other events took place in the Hudson River area. However, the British were never able to seize the important waterway. Historians believe that the British failure to control the Hudson was a key reason for their defeat.

### THE MOHAWK RIVER

The Mohawk River, which is 148 miles (237 kilometers) long, is the chief tributary, or branch, of the Hudson River. Before the opening of the Erie Canal, the Mohawk was the main passageway to the west. Despite the river's rapids, falls, and shallows, natives, merchants, army troops, and settlers all used the Mohawk to move between New York and the Great Lakes region. The river was so important in the late eighteenth century that the Western Inland Lock Navigation Company was formed to improve the Mohawk waterway.

## Steamboats and a Canal

In 1807, Robert Fulton piloted the first steamboat up the Hudson River. The *Clermont* made the trip from New York City to Albany in thirty-two hours, a record for the time. The steamboat was a milestone in river transportation. People journeying up the Hudson no longer had to worry about the wind or the rapids. As the steamboat became more efficient, it became faster. Eventually, a trip from one end of the river to the other took just eight hours. The steamboat was also one of the most affordable ways to travel. By 1850, there were 150 steamboats on the river.

With the advent of the railroad, steamboating decreased somewhat. The first railroad, opened in 1831, was the Mohawk and Hudson Line, which ran between Albany and Schenectady. By the early 1850s, a train ride between Albany and New York City took only four hours—half the time of a steamboat ride.

*The Empire State Express thunders through Break-neck Mountain on its way to New York City in November 1941.*

# The Erie Canal

In 1825, the opening of the Erie Canal ushered in a new era for the Hudson. The canal opened a water route from the Great Lakes all the way to the Atlantic Ocean. It connected Buffalo on Lake Erie to Albany on the Hudson River. From Albany, goods were shipped down the Hudson to New York.

The Hudson soon became a river of national importance, serving as a passageway to the west. Later, the Delaware and Hudson Canal linked New York to the coal mines of Pennsylvania. The Champlain Canal was used to transport lumber from Lake Champlain down to the Hudson River.

The man behind the Erie Canal was New York's governor, DeWitt Clinton. At first, Clinton tried to get federal funding for his pet project. When that failed, he convinced state lawmakers that the state of New York should pay for the canal. Work on the project began in Rome, New York, in 1817.

When the canal was finished, it measured 363 miles (581 kilometers) long, 40 feet (12 meters) wide, and an average of 4 feet (1.2 meters) deep. Officials celebrated by boating from Buffalo to New York City. At New York, a barrel of Lake Erie water was poured into the Atlantic Ocean.

The Erie Canal encouraged the growth of many businesses along the river, such as brick factories, mills, iron foundries, and firearms factories. The canal also made it easier for immigrants who landed in New York City to migrate to the west. Over the years, more than 20 million immigrants entered the United States through New York City's port. Thousands of them used the canal to continue their journey into the nation's interior.

Until the 1850s, the Erie Canal was the best way to get goods from one place to another in New York. However, the railroads soon caused canal traffic to decrease. The opening of the St. Lawrence Seaway in 1959 also hurt the canal.

## HUDSON RIVERKEEPER

Since 1983, the Hudson River has been carefully monitored by riverkeepers. Riverkeepers are people who patrol the Hudson by boat. The riverkeepers are hired and organized by Riverkeeper, Inc., an environmental group that is concerned about the Hudson's future. Riverkeepers check water quality and make sure that people, ships, and industries do not pollute the river. In recent years, about fifty riverkeeper programs have sprung up around the United States.

*"Moonlight" by Ralph Albert Blakelock is done in the Hudson River school–style of landscape painting. This style of painting is sometimes referred to as "romantic realism." It was practiced by artists from 1825 to 1870.*

# Pollution and Preservation

In the twentieth century, industrial waste and other pollution began taking their toll on the Hudson River. Trash, sewage, and chemicals spewed into the water, depleting fish supplies and damaging water quality.

In recent years, people who care about the Hudson have joined to make sure that the river can be enjoyed by future generations. Community and environmental groups have worked to clean and protect the river. In 1996, Congress named the Hudson River valley a National Heritage Area. This is a National Park Service designation that recognizes sites of natural, cultural, historic, and scenic value. In the coming years, the state of New York will spend millions of dollars to make sure that the Hudson River remains healthy.

# Lake Champlain

**9**

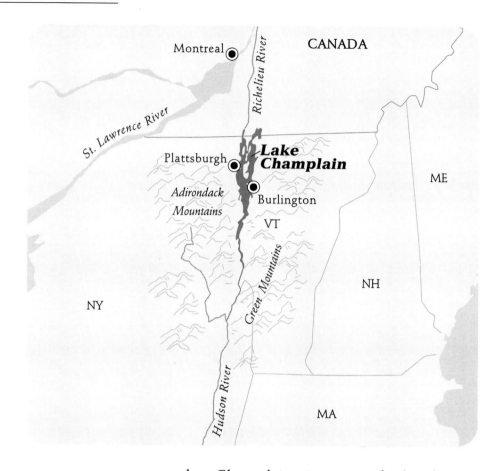

**L**ake Champlain is one of the largest freshwater lakes in the United States. The lake forms part of the boundary between New York and Vermont and stretches a few miles into Canada. It measures about 120 miles (192 kilometers) in length and between 0.5 miles and 12 miles (0.8 kilometers and 19.2 kilometers) in width. The lake covers an area of 435 square miles (1,131 square kilometers) and is 400 feet (120 meters) deep in some parts. Average depths, however, are about 64 feet (19.2 meters).

The lake's waters flow from south to north, emptying into the Richelieu River in Quebec. The Richelieu then connects to the St. Lawrence River, which empties into the Atlantic Ocean. Several important rivers empty into Lake Champlain.

Lake Champlain is a beautiful, scenic place. The lake is sandwiched between the Adirondack Mountains to the west and the Green Mountains to the east. More than seventy islands dot the lake itself, including Grande Isle, Isle La Motte, and Valcour Island.

Lake Champlain has played an important role in America's early history. During three early wars in America, the lake was an important battle site. Native Americans, French, British, and Americans all struggled for control of the lake region during the nation's development.

# Settlement

The first people to settle in the area were Native American tribes, including the Iroquois, Abenaki, and Algonquin people. These people hunted in the woods, grew crops on the lake's shore, and fished in the lake. They also used the lake as a pathway to the Hudson River to trade with other tribes, as well as to wage war with one another.

The first European to explore the lake was Frenchman Samuel de Champlain. In 1609, Champlain and his band visited the area with a group of Algonquin people. Their mission was to defeat the Iroquois, the traditional enemies of the Algonquin. Champlain's visit and his alliance with the Algonquin people created hostility between the French and the Iroquois that would continue for a long time.

For many years after Champlain's visit, the lake was left to the Iroquois. The first settlement on the lake was Fort Ste. Anne, built in 1666 by the French. The fort, constructed on what is now Isle La Motte, was built to give explorers from New France (Canada) a place to rest before heading south. The French destroyed the fort just three years later when they abandoned the island and returned to Canada.

Once the British took control of the region in the late 1700s, colonists from the East Coast began heading into the area. One of the earliest settlements in the region was Burlington, Vermont, founded in 1763 on the eastern shore of Lake Champlain. Another early settlement was Skenesborough, New York, founded on the western shore in 1764 by Philip Skene.

Today, many people live along the lake's shores. Burlington and South Burlington, Vermont, are the largest cities on the lake's eastern shore. Plattsburgh and Crown Point, New York, are the largest on the western shore.

## A SIXTH GREAT LAKE?

In 1998, an effort was made in the U.S. Congress to declare Lake Champlain America's sixth Great Lake. Area lawmakers knew that if Champlain became one of the Great Lakes, it would receive more government funding for research and education. In February 1998, a bill that named Lake Champlain as a Great Lake was passed by both the House of Representatives and the Senate. However, the designation was taken away just weeks later. Opponents of the bill pointed out that Lake Champlain is not connected by any natural waterways to the rest of the Great Lakes. Champlain is also only about one-sixteenth the size of Lake Ontario, the smallest of the Great Lakes.

## Commerce and Travel

The earliest European settlers in the Lake Champlain area planted crops and erected sawmills and gristmills near the lake. They quickly realized that the key to prosperity in the region lay with shipping and trade. Soon, shipbuilding businesses sprang up along the lake's shores. The ships were used to carry goods to the north and the south.

One town on Lake Champlain became well known as a shipbuilding center. In the early 1800s, Vergennes, Vermont, was home to the Macdonough Shipyard and the Lake Champlain Steamboat Company. During the War of 1812 (1812–1815), the USS *Saratoga* was built at the Macdonough yard. For the Americans, this battleship would be crucial in winning the Battle of Lake Champlain.

Timber was another important natural resource. Wood that was not used to build homes and other buildings was burned, and its ashes were used to create a substance called *potash*. Potash was used to fertilize crops and to make glass and soap. Iron was also mined in the area for a short time.

*The paddlewheel steamship Champlain II ran aground on the rocks near Westport, New York, on Lake Champlain in 1875. It was never salvaged and became the first New York State Submerged Heritage Preserve.*

## A New Era on the Lake

In 1808, a new invention transformed boating on Lake Champlain. That year, the world's second steamship, the *Vermont*, began chugging across the lake. In 1832, the lake economy got another big boost when the Champlain Canal was completed. The canal linked Lake Champlain with the Hudson River and the Atlantic Ocean. Such lake cities as Burlington became centers of commerce and trade, shipping lake products and receiving finished goods to and from New York City.

*Sailboats move across the starting line during the fourteenth annual M.S. Regatta on Lake Champlain. Water sports of all types are an important part of the economy of the Lake Champlain area.*

Today, tourism is an important part of the Lake Champlain economy. Numerous resorts and cottages border the lake, offering sun and fun. Swimming, boating, fishing, and other summertime activities draw thousands of visitors every year. Each summer, the area's population soars as part-time residents return to this beautiful area.

# Warfare on the Lake

Lake Champlain's location and the rivers connecting it to both Canada and the United States made it a strategic piece of territory to early American and Canadian settlers. French and English explorers quickly realized that the lake's waters were important to controlling the Northeast. Over the years, hundreds of Native Americans, French, English, and Americans have died trying to control the lake region. Numerous battleships lie below the lake's surface.

Even before Europeans arrived, the Lake Champlain area was the scene of conflict and battle. The Iroquois claimed the lake, as did the Huron and Algonquin peoples. War parties carrying out bloody attacks from these tribes were common. However, these skirmishes were small compared to the bloodshed that the area would see in the 1700s.

# The French and Indian War

In 1689, the British and French began struggling for control of North America. The Lake Champlain area was an important battleground during the final phase of that conflict, called the French and Indian War (1754–1763). The French used the lake to move south into British territory, while the British used the same strategy to advance into Canada.

During the course of the war, both the French and the British built forts along Lake Champlain's shores. One of the most famous was Ticonderoga (tie-con-dah-ROH-gah), a stone fort built between Lake Champlain and Lake George to the south. The fort was constructed in 1755 by the French. They called their new outpost Carillon. In 1758, the British attacked in one of the bloodiest battles of the war. When the British finally captured the fort the following year, they renamed it

Ticonderoga, which comes from an Iroquois term meaning "where the waters meet."

In 1763, the British took control of the colonies and drove the French from all the land in North America east of the Mississippi. This marked the end of the war and the end of a French empire in the New World.

# The American Revolution

From Montreal and Quebec, the British had the perfect entry point into the heart of the rebelling American colonies during the American Revolution (1775–1783). By advancing south from Canada and north from New York Bay, the British hoped to regain control of the United States. The pathway between the two points, running through the Lake Champlain area, soon became known as the "Great Warpath."

Even before the American Revolution officially started, Fort Ticonderoga in New York came under attack. Ethan Allen and his Green Mountain Boys captured the fort from the British. Allen was an American patriot from Vermont. His troops of soldiers were named for the Green Mountains of that state. The British recaptured the fort two years later and managed to hold on to it until the end of the war.

In the fall of 1776, an important battle took place on Lake Champlain. On October 11, American commander Benedict Arnold sailed a small fleet of fifteen ships into the middle of the lake. The ships had been hastily put together by shipbuilders and farmers in Vermont. Arnold and his sailors were up against a huge British fleet of more than 640 vessels on their way from Canada to take New York City. Although the tiny American fleet was destroyed, it put up a brave fight. This fierce battle between the Royal Navy and a group of determined patriots discouraged the British and caused them to return to Canada.

## BENEDICT ARNOLD: FROM HERO TO TRAITOR

In the early stages of the American Revolution (1775–1783), Benedict Arnold distinguished himself as an American hero and patriot. Arnold helped capture Fort Ticonderoga, held off the British on Lake Champlain, and helped lead the Americans to victory at Saratoga, New York. But by the late 1770s, Arnold's thoughts had turned to treason.

Badly in debt and bitter after being passed over for promotion in the Continental Army, Arnold decided to cut a deal with the British. In 1778, he plotted with the British to surrender West Point, an important American fort on the Hudson River. In exchange, Arnold was to receive money and a top position in the British army. The plot was discovered by the Americans, however, and Arnold was forced to flee to the British.

As a general in the British army, Arnold led raids against his former compatriots. In 1781, Arnold and his men attacked Richmond, Virginia, and New London, Connecticut, burning ships and buildings and killing many colonial troops. Later that year, Arnold sailed to England with his family. Even in England, however, he was considered a traitor and turncoat. He died there in 1801, his name forever linked with treason and treachery.

*This 1776 drawing depicts the Battle of Valcour Island between British forces and the smaller American fleet, commanded by General Benedict Arnold. Arnold was commodore of the American fleet on Lake Champlain.*

# The War of 1812

Lake Champlain once again became an arena of battle during the War of 1812, when 14,000 British troops invaded the lake area from Canada. Their ultimate goal was to capture New York City. On September 11, 1814, American forces gathered off the shore of Plattsburgh, New York, ready to take on the invaders.

The Battle of Lake Champlain was one of the key battles of the war. Commodore Thomas Macdonough defeated the British, sending them fleeing from the lake region for the last time. Never again would the British attempt to use the area as the "Great Warpath."

*This etching shows the USS* Constitution *exchanging fire with the British ship* Guerriere *on Lake Champlain on August 19, 1812. The* Guerriere *was destroyed after only thirty minutes of battle.*

# Today

In recent years, Lake Champlain has faced a threat of a different kind. The zebra mussel, a nonnative species, has infested the lake. These pesky, hard-shelled creatures were first discovered in Lake Champlain in 1993. They spread from the Great Lakes

# CHAMP,
# THE LAKE CHAMPLAIN MONSTER

Everyone has heard of the Loch Ness monster, but did you know that Lake Champlain may have a strange creature of its own? "Champ" is said to be a snakelike animal 30 feet (9 meters) long. This mysterious lake monster has supposedly been spotted more than 130 times since the early 1800s.

The first people to see this local legend were native peoples who lived in the area. The Abanaki told tales of a strange lake creature that they called "Tatoskok." One of the first sightings by early settlers occurred in New York in 1819.

In the 1870s, a number of sightings were reported. In 1871, passengers on a lake steamer saw the head of a strange creature with a long neck. According to witnesses, Champ left a 30- to 40-foot (9- to 12-meter) wake behind it. In 1873, a railroad crew spotted the gigantic beast. That same year, famous showman P.T. Barnum offered a $50,000 reward to anyone who could supply him with the creature's hide.

Interest in Champ peaked in the 1970s. In 1979, Joseph Zarzynski founded the Lake Champlain Phenomena Investigation to search out evidence of Champ's existence. Zarzynski believes that there is enough proof to say that *something* is swimming below the lake's surface. In 1982 and 1983, Vermont and New York passed resolutions protecting Champ—if there is such a creature.

through canals and other waterways to Lake Champlain. Zebra mussels cause problems by attaching themselves to any hard surfaces, including boat hulls and engines. They also clog water intake and purification pipes.

Zebra mussels affect water quality and disrupt the lake ecosystem by competing with native species for food. They are also destroying some of Lake Champlain's history by damaging the wooden shipwrecks lying beneath the lake surface. Today, twenty-three stations have been set up around Lake

Champlain to monitor the population of zebra mussels and their effects on the lake.

Water pollution has also been a problem in the lake in recent years. Such pollutants as sewage, fertilizers, and other waste products caused the water quality in Lake Champlain to decline. Stricter regulations for polluting industries and state aid have helped the lake begin to recover.

# New York Bay

10

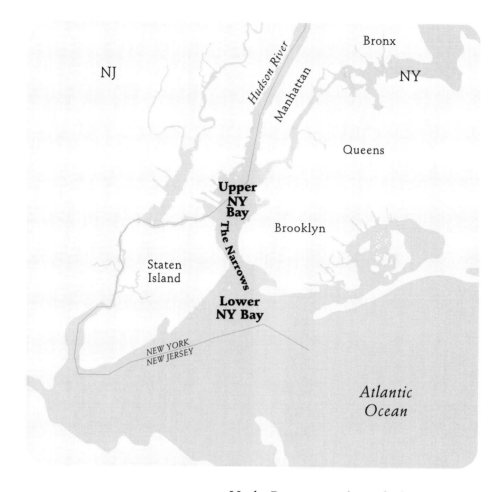

**N**ew York Bay, an inlet of the Atlantic Ocean, is located in southeastern New York. The bay is surrounded by the New York City boroughs of Manhattan, Brooklyn, and Staten Island, as well as part of New Jersey's northeastern coast. The Upper Bay and Lower Bay are separated by the Narrows, a thin section of the bay that separates Manhattan and Staten Island.

Although it is not one of the largest bays in the United States, New York Bay is certainly one of the most important. Since the early 1600s, the bay has played an integral part in the shaping of the United States. New York Bay has been central to the nation's economic and cultural growth. The United States can trace its great ethnic diversity directly to the bay, too:

For nearly 400 years, New York Bay has served as one of the gateways to America for millions of immigrants from every part of the world.

## The History of the Bay

The first people to inhabit the bay region were Native Americans who arrived as long ago as 10,000 years. Later, many native tribes lived in the area. These tribes included the Manhattan, Lenape, Mahican, and Rockaway. The tribes hunted and fished in the bay area and grew crops of beans, squash, and corn.

The first European to enter New York Bay was Giovanni da Verrazano (gee-oh-VAHN-ee dah ver-rah-ZAHN-oh) in 1524. Verrazano was an Italian who was sailing under the flag of France. He did not claim the land for the French, leaving the way clear for Henry Hudson and the Dutch in 1609. That year, Hudson, an Englishman, explored the bay region, sailing about 150 miles (240 kilometers) up the Hudson River before turning back. He took glowing reports of the area and its potential riches back to the Netherlands.

In 1625, the Dutch West India Company, a group of Dutch merchants, established the first trading post on New York Bay. A permanent settlement followed in 1626. New Amsterdam, as the town was called, was at the southern tip of Manhattan Island.

New Amsterdam was a trading town. The settlers there traded blankets, beads, and other trinkets to the local natives for animal furs. They sent back to the Netherlands beaver, otter, mink, and fox skins to be made into hats and other articles of clothing.

> • Fast Fact •
> The name Manhattan comes from the native word **mannahata,** which may mean "island of hills."

From the beginning, the new settlement was a place of cultural diversity. The Dutch merchants were happy to welcome all who wanted to settle, no matter what their religion or nationality might be. In 1654, there were immigrants speaking more than fifteen different languages in New Amsterdam.

The only people who were not tolerated were the natives of the region. As the fur trade slowed, bay area settlers turned to farming. They began moving northward, pushing the Lenapes and other native tribes off their land in order to have more land to farm. By the end of the eighteenth century, most of the natives who had once lived around New York Bay were gone, either killed off by disease or in battles with the new settlers or forced to move away.

As more and more settlers arrived in the area, they looked for land all around the bay, not just on Manhattan. Brooklyn, for example, was founded by the Dutch in 1635. Settlers moved between Manhattan and Brooklyn by rowboat. In 1639, Danish captain Jonas Bronck moved to an area north of Manhattan. The area would soon be known as "the Broncks," later, the "Bronx."

Dutch control of the area did not last long. In 1664, four British ships sailed into New York Bay and claimed the area for Great Britain. The Dutch, with little means to defend the region, quietly surrendered. New Amsterdam was renamed New York in honor of James, Duke of York (later King James II). The city was poised to become one of the most important trade centers in the world.

## ISLAND FOR SALE?

In 1624, Dutchman Peter Minuit bought Manhattan Island from the native Manhattan tribe. Minuit purchased the 14,000 acres (5,600 hectares) with items that may have included axes, farm tools, cloth, and trinkets. The value of the goods was estimated to be sixty Dutch guilders. In today's dollars, that sum would equal more than $650. The natives had no idea that they were selling away the rights to their land forever.

## STREETS OF NEW YORK

In 1653, the Dutch in New Amsterdam erected a wall to protect them from English and native attacks from the north. The 2,340-foot (702-meter) wall stretched from Manhattan's east shore to the west shore. In 1699, the wall was torn down and replaced with a road that the English named Wall Street.

Broadway, from the Dutch *Breede Wegh*, was once a native hunting trail. The Dutch widened it in the 1600s to facilitate trade with the natives.

In 1811, a special commission came up with a plan to develop the streets of northern Manhattan in an orderly fashion. The commission mapped out a grid of more than 2,000 nearly identical blocks. New streets were all neatly numbered.

*Times Square, in the heart of New York City, is one of the busiest places on Earth. Its famed billboards and other lighted signs can be seen on television each New Year's Eve, when thousands of people pack the streets.*

# A Capital of Commerce

With the arrival of the English, a new era began for the New York Bay area. The bay soon became one of the busiest ports in the colonies, sending ships full of goods to other world ports. New York colonists shipped wheat, tobacco, and timber. Ships returned with molasses, sugar, ivory, and other goods. By the early 1740s, New York was the third-largest port in the world.

Trade in slaves was also an important part of New York's shipping business. In New York, the Dutch had begun the practice of bringing enslaved people from Africa to the colonies. In 1827, this practice was finally banned by state law.

# The American Revolution (1775–1783)

As unrest between Britain and the American colonies grew, people in New York became uneasy. They knew that New York Bay, with its central location on the Atlantic seaboard, would be a key target for the British. Once war was declared in 1775, General George Washington and all New Yorkers began preparing for the assault that they knew would come.

## REVOLUTIONARY FACTS

- During the Battle of Long Island, one out of every four colonial soldiers that took part in the battle was killed.
- About 11,000 colonial troops died in British prison ships anchored in New York Bay.
- On November 25, 1783, Manhattan became the last piece of colonial territory to be surrendered by the British.
- New York was the capital of the United States from 1785 to 1790.
- George Washington was inaugurated as the nation's first president in Manhattan.

That assault took place on August 27, 1776. In the Battle of Long Island, the British attacked and easily captured Brooklyn. In November, the British siege of the area was complete when they marched into Manhattan.

During the seven years of the war, the New York Bay area remained under British control. Over the course of the war, Manhattan was devastated. Many buildings burned to the ground; others were abandoned. The thriving trade industry that had helped the city prosper came to a halt.

## Boom Years for the Bay

Although Manhattan had been left in ruins after the war, people quickly returned to pick up the pieces. Within two years, the city's population had returned to its prewar numbers, and trade was booming.

In 1825, the completion of the Erie Canal made the bay one of the most important harbors in the world. The canal provided a link between the Great Lakes and the Atlantic Ocean. Goods from the West, instead of being shipped down the Mississippi River to New Orleans, were now funneled down the Hudson River to the ports in New York's bay.

**A CAPITAL OF CULTURE**

New York City is known throughout the world as a capital of culture. Residents and visitors have a host of cultural opportunities to choose from, including museums, art galleries, operas, concerts, and even one of the most famous amusement parks in the United States: Coney Island in Brooklyn. One of the most well-known areas of the city is Broadway, where people can see plays and musicals in any of the more than thirty theaters located there.

As the shipping and trade businesses boomed, other industries grew up around them. The New York Stock Exchange (NYSE) began in the 1790s under a buttonwood tree in Manhattan. Men would meet under the tree to trade stocks and government bonds. In 1836, the stock exchange moved to its new headquarters on Wall Street. Today, millions of stocks are bought and sold through the NYSE every day.

Other important industries that grew up in New York City include clothes making, publishing, and retail sales. Today, New York is still a center of these industries. New York is noted around the world as a center for fashion. Dozens of major book, magazine, and newspaper publishers are located in New York. And millions of shoppers visit such famous stores as Saks Fifth Avenue, Macy's, Bloomingdale's, and F.A.O. Schwarz.

# Migration and New York City

Beginning in the 1600s, immigrants trickled into New York's bay area, looking for refuge. In the 1830s, the trickle turned into a flood. Many of these first immigrants came from Ireland and Germany. Later groups came from Italy, Poland, and many other Eastern European countries. From 1892 to 1943, more than 12 million immigrants passed through the Ellis Island immigration center in New York Bay.

Many of the immigrants moved on. Some of them took steamships up the Hudson to the Erie Canal and traveled to the West. Others journeyed up or down the Atlantic seaboard. Most, however, stayed and made their homes in New York City.

The immigrants provided a plentiful supply of labor for New York's developing industries. Men, women, and children worked long hours sewing shirts, making shoes, digging ditches, and building streets. The hours were long, the pay was poor, and in many factories, working conditions were horrible. The workers' attempts to improve these conditions

eventually led to the establishment of the first labor unions in the United States.

The new arrivals settled in the crowded, old neighborhoods of New York. They lived inside dark, dirty tenement buildings. The packed, filthy conditions of these buildings often led to outbreaks of such diseases as cholera, tuberculosis, and typhus. The problems of the new population spurred the development of health, education, and other social services throughout the area.

## IMMIGRATION AND POLITICS

The terrible poverty that many immigrants lived in led to the rise of one of the most corrupt politicians in U.S. history: William "Boss" Tweed. Tweed came to power in the 1860s by offering aid to the city's poorest residents. In return, immigrants needed only to vote for Tweed and his cohorts. But even Tweed's strongest supporters turned against him when they learned that he had been embezzling thousands of dollars from the city.

New York continues to be a gateway to the United States. In the early 1900s, many black Americans moved into the New York bay area seeking employment in area industries. More recently, people have come from Puerto Rico, Cuba, South America, and all parts of Asia to find a better way of life.

# Building Up and Out

The population of Manhattan swelled during the 1800s, and people began looking for ways to create more living and working space. Bridges were built to connect the island with its neighborhoods. The Brooklyn Bridge was the first. Finished in 1883, the bridge connected Manhattan to Brooklyn across the East River. The bridge opened up Brooklyn to the growing number of immigrants coming to America through New York Bay.

The age of the skyscrapers began in the late 1880s. Because of the strength of the city's ancient bedrock, New York was the perfect place for these tall, multistoried buildings. The steel-framed skyscrapers allowed New Yorkers to move upward. The first skyscraper, called the Tower Building, was built in 1889. The race to build the highest structure in New York was on. In 1931, the tallest building in the world was the 102-story Empire State Building.

For many years, the twin peaks of the World Trade Center held the title for the tallest structures in New York. The North Tower measured 1,368 feet (410 meters) in height, while the South Tower was 4 feet (1.2 meters) shorter. Both big buildings towered 110 stories over New York Bay.

As a center for trade and commerce, the Twin Towers also served as symbols of American industry and prosperity. On the morning of September 11, 2001, a terrorist attack brought the buildings crashing down and altered New York's skyline forever.

## LADY LIBERTY

For many immigrants, their first glimpse of the New World was the Statue of Liberty standing proudly in New York Bay. The 151-foot (45.3-meter), 2,225-ton (2,003-metric ton) statue was a gift to the United States from France. On the statue's pedestal, words by New Yorker Emma Lazarus inspired hope: "Give me your tired, your poor, your huddled masses yearning to breathe free."

*Liberty Island and the Statue of Liberty stand in New York Harbor.*

opposite: The Brooklyn Bridge, right, and the Manhattan Bridge span New York's East River, from Manhattan to Brooklyn. On January 1, 1898, five boroughs were fused into the city of New York, increasing its population by 1.4 million in a single day.

The attack began when terrorists took control of a jetliner and crashed it into the North Tower. Less than twenty minutes later, terrorists crashed a second jet into the South Tower. The explosions and raging fires weakened the towers. Less than two hours later, both structures gave way and tumbled to the ground. Nearly 3,000 people were killed, including many firefighters and police officers who had rushed into the buildings to help.

## Getting Around

As the population in Manhattan grew, so did the number of vehicles crowding city streets. City officials recognized the need to provide public transportation. In 1868, the first elevated railway system in the world began operating. New York's last el stopped running in 1955.

In 1904, New York's subway system opened to the public. The subway was much quieter and more efficient than the el. Before long, the subway had eased traffic woes in the busy city and connected Manhattan with its four neighboring boroughs. Over the years, it has offered an inexpensive means of transportation to millions of city dwellers and tourists.

Those who wanted to travel out of the city could use the New York Central Railroad. The New York Central was established by Cornelius Vanderbilt in the 1860s. It linked New York to other major cities, including Boston, Chicago, and Montreal. The line continued operating until 1968, when it merged with the Pennsylvania Railroad.

## FAMOUS BRIDGES AND TUNNELS

The New York bay area is home to some of the most famous passenger bridges and tunnels in the world.

- *Brooklyn Bridge:* The first major bridge in the bay area, the Brooklyn Bridge connects Manhattan and Brooklyn. When it was completed in 1883, it was the longest bridge in the world.

- *Verrazano-Narrows Bridge:* Completed in 1964, the Verrazano-Narrows Bridge connects Brooklyn and Staten Island. One of the longest expansion bridges in the world, the Verrazano-Narrows is 4,260 feet (1,278 meters) long.

- *Holland Tunnel:* When it was completed in 1927, the Holland Tunnel was the first tunnel in New York and the longest in the world. It links Manhattan to New Jersey under the Hudson River.

- *Lincoln Tunnel:* Built between 1937 and 1957, the Lincoln Tunnel also links Manhattan to New Jersey under the Hudson. It is one of the busiest tunnels in the world.

# The Bay Today

New York Bay is still one of the world's most important harbors. It is home to many thriving port cities, and the nation's economic health is closely tied to that of the bay. In addition, millions of people of diverse backgrounds live and work together in the bay area. Today, people from around the world continue to come to New York. Some come as tourists to enjoy the pace of one of the world's most vital cities. Others come to live in an area that still serves as a portal to the United States and a center of economic possibilities.

# Sources

## BOOKS

Aylesworth, Thomas G., and Virginia L. Aylesworth. *Middle Atlantic States (Delaware, Maryland, and Pennsylvania).* New York: Chelsea House, 1990.

Aylesworth, Thomas G., and Virginia L. Aylesworth. *Northern New England (Maine, New Hampshire, and Vermont).* New York: Chelsea House, 1990.

Aylesworth, Thomas G., and Virginia L. Aylesworth. *Southern New England (Connecticut, Massachusetts, and Rhode Island).* New York: Chelsea House, 1990.

Hamner, Trudy J. *Living in the Mountains: A Cultural Geography.* New York: Franklin Watts, 1988.

Lourie, Peter. *Hudson River: An Adventure from the Mountain to the Sea.* Honesdale, Pennsylvania: Boyds Mill Press, 1998.

St. Antoine, Sara, ed. *Stories from Where We Live: The North Atlantic Coast.* Minneapolis: Milkweed Editions, 2000.

## WEB SITES

AdirondackNET *www.adirondack.net*

The Chesapeake Bay Program *www.chesapeakebay.net*

The Environmental Protection Agency's American Heritage Rivers *www.epa.gov/rivers/*

The National Park Service *www.nps.gov*

New York City's official site *www.home.nyc.gov/portal/index/jsp?pageID=nyc_home*

# Index